Memoirs of an Inner City Elementary School Principal

Pat Michaux

authorHOUSE®

AuthorHouse™
1663 Liberty Drive
Bloomington, IN 47403
www.authorhouse.com
Phone: 1-800-839-8640

First published by AuthorHouse on 2011

ISBN: 978-1-4567-5758-8 (e)
ISBN: 978-1-4567-5759-5 (hc)
ISBN: 978-1-4567-5760-1 (sc)

Library of Congress Control Number: 2011904572

Printed in the United States of America

Acknowledgments

I would like to express my gratitude to the following:

The writing classes at the Carnegie Center in Lexington, Kentucky.

To Leatha Kendrick, the first editor of Memoirs, who laughed, cried, and edited the chapters of Memoir. Our meetings at the Great Harvest Bread Company in Palomar Center were a delight. We drank coffee and ate the mouth watering bread of the day! Thank you, Leatha, for your time and wisdom.

To Susan DuArte, who edited, proof read, edited, and proof read some more to make the Memoirs come alive to the readers. Thank you, Susan, for your time and energy to get the book to the publishing stage!

To my family and friends who had to listen to my stories over the years whether they wanted to or not! I am forever indebted to your patience in listening to me and your words of encouragement to get the book published.

Contents

Prologue

My memoir journey began during the 1985-'86 school year. This was when I was selected as principal of Johnson Elementary School which was located in the inner city of Lexington, Kentucky.

This book contains notes of activities, stories, events, and many home visits.

I pay tribute to the staff who stayed with me as their principal for sixteen years, along with local businesses, organizations, local churches, Southland Christian Church, private citizens, University of Kentucky, Transylvania University, Georgetown University, and the Fayette County Board of Education who supported Johnson School.

All names of the students and parents have been fictionalized. Real names were used in newspaper articles, letters, events, and programs.

I recognize and thank two deceased people who deeply touched me during my years at Johnson Elementary. They were Mrs. Rebecca Wheat Hall Sutton- my mother, and Mrs. Emma Price, neighbor and friend, who lived across the street from the school.

Enjoy the memoirs!

The Early Years

The dated Chevy van coughed and sputtered as the motor stopped. I parked across the street in front of Johnson Elementary School. Six beige painted concrete windows surrounded by old red brick faced me. The only visible landscaping was one lone tree struggling to survive near the flagpole. The place looked like a prison in the inner city, not a school.

On the wide steps to the school's entrance sat a mother and four children.

"Hello!" I said as I approached them.

"Who the hell are you?" The mother asked.

"I'm the new principal of Johnson Elementary School," I replied.

She said, "I hope you don't give my kids head lice and send them home like that other principal did."

"I sure hope I don't either," I answered.

It was the July 1985-86 school year in Lexington, Kentucky. I was happy to be at Johnson Elementary School, I thought, as I walked into the school and main office.

All of the years of additional education for Master of Education degrees, and Rank I in Administration had been worth the blood, sweat, and tears! I was a physical education teacher for eighteen years in Kentucky and now was in a new position as principal of Johnson Elementary School.

Changing my wardrobe from sweat suits and sneakers to business suits, pantyhose, and heels turned out to be my first challenge. I had finally arrived as principal of my own school. I spent most of my morning reading through the curriculum, schedules, budget, and staff roster. Before lunch, I decided to meet some of the families in the community since the teachers were not starting back to school until the next week.

As I walked up and down Sixth Street, knocking on doors, hoping to introduce myself as the new principal, no one opened a door to greet me. TVs were on but no face appeared at the door.

Frustrated, I returned to the school, called the previous principal and said, "The people here aren't friendly. I walked up and down Sixth Street trying to introduce myself as the new principal but no one would come to the door."

I heard a deep belly laugh, and the principal said, "Michaux, they thought you were a new girl (prostitute) on the street." I was dumbfounded! I had no idea there were prostitutes in the city much less out walking in broad daylight near a school.

I later learned that Sixth Street was part of the "stroll" where "hookers" walked, and worked during the day, and on into the wee hours of the night. The "stroll" was a four block square- Sixth Street to Martin Luther King Street, to Third Street, up Limestone, and back to Sixth.

* * *

During my first year at Johnson Elementary, I spent many hours learning the budget and its different codes for spending allocated funds. I was thankful that the secretary explained what each code represented. Money from each code was spent only for certain items. Fee money for supplies was a real concern because we needed more supplies through the year than we had money to pay for in the budget.

Before the school year started, the teachers came a day early, had a staff meeting, organized their rooms with new school supplies, decorated the class bulletin boards, and met with their grade level colleagues on curriculum schedules.

Before our staff meeting in the morning, I asked the cafeteria manager to have breakfast served in the cafeteria for the staff. The cafeteria manager and her staff provided an excellent meal, paid for out of my pocket, since there was no money for team building or boosting morale. The teachers appreciated it. I believed in using school cafeteria personnel for all food functions when possible.

At the first staff meeting, I said, "Please share something positive about your summer vacation."

Several of the teachers shared funny stories about their adventures. Laughter hung in the air.

I said," Please share some of your concerns as a teacher at Johnson School."

Some teachers bemoaned the lack of supplies through the school year. Others said, "Our parents aren't involved in the children's education as much as we would like them to be. Lice and truancy are big problems here."

I had not experienced any of these concerns in my previous schools, at least not to the extent these teachers were describing at Johnson.

The rest of the day, as teachers worked in their rooms, I visited each classroom. In one teacher's room, the closet was full of faded construction paper and extra glue bottles.

"Why weren't these items used for students last year?" I asked.

She replied, "Because I was afraid I wouldn't have enough supplies for this year."

"Please use the supplies purchased this year on your students. The state funds are to be used for the students you have in your room this year. I'll make sure you have the supplies you need next year," I said.

In my opinion, principals needed to support the staff with supplies throughout the school year and not make them buy supplies out of pocket. Teachers needed to concentrate on teaching the curriculum and should not have to worry about funding for additional supplies, workbooks, and paper.

Observing how school supplies were handled in previous years, I discovered that the few surplus supplies were kept locked in an office closet. The secretary had the only key.

Before the first day of school, as teachers were preparing their classrooms for their students, a teacher came into the office. She asked the secretary for a box of paperclips. The secretary said, "No."

I was standing in the office and said, "Why can't she have a box of paperclips?"

The secretary said, "She got a box of paperclips with her August supplies. She cannot have another box until our winter supply order comes in January."

I had never heard of such a thing! At my previous school, the teachers got whatever supplies they needed. "Give the teacher a box of paperclips, anyway," I said. The secretary got upset with me, but I felt that if a teacher needed more paperclips, she should get them.

* * *

On the first day of the new school year, I helped enroll new students in Johnson Elementary School.

One father gave me "911" as an emergency number to call in case his child got sick or hurt.

"I cannot accept this number," I said.

He said, "Sure you can. If my kid gets sick or hurt, call 911 and pick me up on the way to the emergency room."

"I can't do that either," I replied." If your child gets sick or hurt, I'll make a home visit, and return you to school to get your child. Then you can decide what you want to do."

Several students arrived without updated immunizations or school supplies. A five-year old student could not stay at school without an immunization card from a doctor's office or the health department, although several students enrolled without either.

"My child must go to school," one parent said.

The nurse said, "Your child has no updated immunizations. You must call the health department and make an appointment for him."

"I have to walk to the health department. It's over a mile from my place." the mother said. She grabbed her child and left, upset that her child couldn't stay. The school nurse found several students with head lice who had to be sent home on the first day.

I was astounded at the barriers the parents faced when enrolling their children in school. The other schools where I taught didn't seem to have as many problems as our Johnson parents had. There had to be a better solution for our students starting the new school year.

* * *

During my years at a suburban school, as a physical education teacher, our P.T.A. (Parent Teacher Association) raised thirty thousand dollars profit for a school fund raiser, each year. The teachers were asked what supplies they needed for the classroom, and the P.T.A. funds were used to buy them. I had the best-equipped storage room in the gymnasium for every activity, sport, movement, or fitness activity available to elementary students in Fayette County.

At Johnson Elementary, the P.T.O. (Parent Teacher Organization) raised forty-one hundred dollars profit every year from the carnival. For our school fund raiser, the students sold candy bars during the first five years that I was principal. However, some of the students' candy money was used to pay bills at home, and a few children ate their candy which affected the school's profit.

As the principal, I was concerned about the safety of the students selling candy bars door to door in the inner city. The parents were supposed to accompany the children or have the candy sold at a parent's place of work. They could also let the grandparents help sell it. Some parents stood in front of a local grocery store and sold candy. The students who sold the most candy earned a nice prize. The top three candy sellers got to ride in a limousine with a staff member and eat lunch at a fast food restaurant.

When Johnson School had half-day kindergarten in the 1980's, the parents were at the school by 11:45 a.m. to pick up their children. When the limousine for the candy winners drove into the school turnaround, the first year, at 11:45a.m., the kindergarten mothers asked me if they could look inside a real limo.

I said, "Better still, let's get in it, and sit down." We all crammed into the limo. They "oohed" and "ahhed" and giggled like children. The limousine was a good learning experience for me. I assumed that when we became adults we had all experienced a limo ride. I had a lot to learn.

* * *

When one mother of a kindergarten student didn't show up at 12:00 noon, to pick up her child, I made a home visit and talked about it with the mother.

"You aren't picking Wanda up on time from school. Instead, you either come at 10:00 a.m. or 1:00p.m. You must come to school by noon. This is the third time we've talked about this problem."

"I can't tell time," the mother said. (Stupid me. I had no clue.)

"Do you watch "The Price Is Right" on T.V?" I asked.

"Yes." she replied.

"O.K, before the three doors open at the end of the show, you start walking to school. You'll be there on time to pick Wanda up."

"Thank you," she said. That worked for a while until her T.V. went on the blink. Then she was either early or late picking Wanda up at school.

Frustrated, I made a home visit again, and said, "You have to be on time to pick Wanda up."

"Ms. Show, I sure do like your red polka dot dress." I thought she was changing the subject on purpose. She had talked about my red dress several times.

I said, "I tell you what; I'll make a deal with you since you and I are about the same size. If you can find a neighbor who will tell you when it is time to pick Wanda up at school, and you do it on time for two weeks, I'll give you my dress."

5

She jumped up and down and said, "I can do it!"

After two weeks of being on time picking Wanda up, I gave her my red dress.

She walked the "stroll" at night. I often wondered if my red dress saw any action.

* * *

It was the middle of September when a parent enrolled her daughter at Johnson School from another county. She was six years old, had completed kindergarten the year before, and was beginning first grade. The mother said they had had a hard time moving, and she didn't get around to enrolling her daughter anywhere. The mother said, "Can I talk to you in secret?"

"Yes," I replied, and took her into my office. I closed the door while her daughter sat in the main office.

"Rhonda wears a 32B bra and the doctor said she could start her period anytime." I was confused because her daughter was short, obese, and still had baby teeth. I visualized her in the primary bathroom changing sanitary pads and was very concerned.

"What did the doctor say was her problem?" I asked.

"Well, when she was two years old she started growing boobs so I took her to the University of Kentucky Hospital .The doctor wanted to give her shots to stop her growin' too fast, and I said no, 'cause I thought she'd be a midget."

Still concerned, I said, "Does your daughter have under arm hair or pubic hair?"

The mother replied, "Girl, she has pubicles all over her body. I have to watch her around the men because they like her. They liked me too when I was her size."

Totally confused at our conversation I asked, "Did you have the same condition growing up that she has?"

She said, "Hell no. I was just fat. Men like fat little girls." I made no comment. Rhonda was a delightful first grader for the three weeks she was with us. Then the family moved to another county.

* * *

One School Record's Day when neither students nor teachers were at school, the secretary and I were talking in the front office. The head custodian came in with three brothers who were Johnson students.

"They were out on the playground early this morning. They said they had no food at home. Are there some chores they can do for food?"

"Didn't you tell me there was a lot of paper on the playground that needs to be picked up?" I asked.

"Yes, there is, come to think of it," he replied.

Before anyone could say anything, the boys said, "We can pick up all the paper!"

Each brother got a pair of rubber gloves and a plastic bag and left. I drove to the grocery store and bought three kinds of cereal and a big jug of milk. We had paper cereal bowls and plastic spoons at school. The boys finished their chores in record time and came to the office to eat. They ate several bowls of cereal and milk. The librarian, who came into the office to copy paperwork, commented, "That cereal sure looks good."

The secretary said, "I was thinking the same thing."

"Fix yourselves a bowl," I offered.

One of the brothers said, "They can't have the cereal. That's ours!"

"No, it belongs to all of us," I replied.

"Oh," he said.

When the students were full they took the rest of the cereal and milk home. The next school day one of the brothers came to the office and said, "You come get us when you need anything done around here."

* * *

Many mornings during my first year as principal, I stood at the entrance of Johnson School and greeted the parents and student walkers.

"Hi, Miss Show!" exclaimed Liza.

"Hi Liza. I'm glad you came to school today," I said, as I picked her up out of a grocery cart. I got my daily hug with her pudgy arms wrapped around my neck. Her mother Mary's toothless smile showed as she held onto the cart handle. It was a two-block walk from their apartment to the school steps.

Mary always wore a muu muu to cover her heavy frame. Her size thirteen slippers had duck heads on top of each shoe. As Mary waddled down the street the duck heads shook from side to side. "I got my shoes at the Goodwill store. Thems the only ones to fit my fat feet," she said.

"Thank you, Mary, for getting Liza to school." I said, as I walked

Liza into the school building, and downstairs to her Educably Mentally Handicapped class. Liza was six years old with an I.Q. of sixty-five.

On rainy days Liza wore a plastic garbage bag over her whole body, with only her face visible. Mary wore a plastic grocery bag over the top of her head. (Most of my students didn't have umbrellas or raincoats.)

One morning, Liza came to school with a big rope tied around her waist, and the other end tied to the grocery cart. "Mary, Why is Liza tied to the grocery cart?" I asked.

"Miss Show, when I was walking her home from school yesterday, we hit a crack, and the grocery cart fell over. Liza fell on her head. Next time she'll stay put," Mary replied.

A few days later a teacher and I were talking in the office. All of a sudden, in runs Liza.

"Come, Miss Show, come! Toby can't poop! she cried. Not knowing what to expect, I grabbed a pair of rubber gloves and followed Liza downstairs. (All personnel were supposed to wear rubber gloves in an emergency.) The rest of the class was sitting on the floor next to the bathroom door with the teacher assistant.

I said to the assistant, "Please take the children to the classroom."

I walked into the bathroom where big boy Toby was seated on the commode in one of the stalls.

Teacher Hurley was saying, "Push, Toby, push."

Ninety pound six year old Toby said, "Miss Show, I can't poop," as he was grinning, grunting, and rocking back and forth on the commode seat.

Ms. Hurley said, "Toby shoved three crayons into his rectum and two have pushed out. Only one to go."

We heard plop! Toby yelled, "Yea!" The teacher said, "Get some toilet paper, wipe yourself, and then wash your hands," as she and I turned to leave the bathroom. Just then we heard him expel gas as he pulled up his pants. He giggled. We did, too. He washed his hands and went to class. Ms. Hurley thanked me for the moral support. I was glad I didn't have to use the gloves. The nurse comes on Tuesdays and Thursdays for half day. Today was Friday. This was not a 911 call.

* * *

There were many discipline problems with which I dealt on a daily basis while learning the role of principal. One day, a first grade teacher sent a student to the office to ask me to come to her classroom about a behavior problem. (There were no phones in the classrooms at the time.)

Six-year old Monica had to be removed from class after hitting the teacher and two of the students. She refused to leave the class, and also, to come with me to the office. I thanked the rest of the class for ignoring Monica's behavior and staying on task. I picked up her small frame and carried her out of the classroom. She started hitting and kicking me as I walked down the hall. There was a custodial closet nearby. I walked in with Monica and shut the door. It was pitch black. The hitting and kicking immediately ceased. She grabbed my neck and cried, "I'm sorry! I'm sorry! Don't leave me!" "I won't leave you but you must calm down and walk to the office with me," I said. After a few sniffles she said, "O.K."

I opened the closet door, she took my hand, and we calmly walked into my office. I never knew what worked with our students when they were out of control, but the abrupt change of scenery worked this time.

* * *

Seven–year old Alyse was sent to the office with a behavior report. It stated that she had stolen tape and paper clips from her teacher's desk and put them in her backpack to take home. The guidance counselor and I were talking in my office when Alyse appeared. I read the report and said, "Alyse, you cannot steal anything from your teacher or anyone else because it is wrong and against the law." The counselor nodded in agreement. I continued, "If you need supplies you should ask for them, not steal them. Why did you steal from your teacher?"

Alyse looked at me with teary eyes and said, "I took the teacher's things because I want to be a teacher when I grow up and I don't have any stuff at home." The counselor and I softened. I said, "You can work toward getting teacher supplies at home for good behavior and finishing your work at school for the next two weeks. But first, you must not steal anymore."

"O.K," she said. "What kind of supplies do you need at home?" I asked.

Alyse perked up and said, "Well, I already have red pencils, glue, scissors, a ruler, and notepads. I need a teacher's plan book." I was dumbfounded. Alyse had been stealing from her teacher for a long time! She was sent to the S.A.F.E. (Suspension and Failure Eliminated) room to do her work until lunch. The counselor agreed to see Alyse weekly for counseling.

* * *

The kindergarten teacher was concerned about an incident in the boys' bathroom. "One of our boys is smearing poop on the bathroom wall. It has happened twice and no one will confess to doing it," she said.

I thought about it, and said, "Have your assistant take the boys to the bathroom two at a time. Then check the walls when they come out." It was three days before two five–year olds were escorted to the office with the assistant.

She said, "There was poop smeared on the bathroom wall after these two boys came out, and both deny doing it." I thanked her and sat the two boys down in my office.

"Tony, you tell me your side of the story about what happened in the bathroom. Then you can tell yours, Maurice."

Tony said, "I used it, and then Maurice said to look at the poop on the wall."

"I just peed," Maurice whined.

"Tony, you go out into the office and wait until I talk with Maurice," I said, as I closed the office door.

There were big tears in Maurice's eyes. "Maurice, I know you smeared poop on the wall. However, I don't understand how you got it out of the commode and up on the wall."

He quickly said, "With a paper towel!"

"What you did was wrong; you are not to smear poop on the walls ever again. If you do you won't be able to use the our bathrooms at school anymore."

He yelled through teary eyes, "I won't ever do it again." The assistant and the two boys returned to class.

* * *

Discipline problems with parents were a major issue at times. Parents who knew the school rules didn't respect them when they were angry, out of control, or on a substance of some kind. They often barged into the school demanding to be heard. Security was called to diffuse many situations and arrests were made when necessary.

A scary incident happened one day at the end of the school day. (The front school doors were unlocked in the 1980's.) The bus riders had been called and the student walkers were waiting in their classrooms to be dismissed, when a student ran into the office, and yelled, "Come quick! She's gonna kill the teacher!"

I ran down the hall with the student. A teacher stepped into the hall and yelled "Stop running in the hall! Oh, it's you, Ms. Michaux!" "Call Security now!" I said, as I ran past her to the teacher's classroom. I opened the door and saw the teacher and seven student walkers huddled in a corner. One of our Johnson mothers was ranting, raving, throwing books and papers on the floor, turning over desks, and yelling obscenities. She was totally out of control.

"Get out, now!" I yelled at the teacher and students as I got between them and the parent.

The teacher was mortified. She and the students were scared of the mother's erratic behavior. The students ran for the door. "Me, too?" asked the teacher.

"Yes! Everyone get out now! I yelled.

Teachers were not trained to deal with this kind of behavior. I was not trained either, but the safety of the students and staff was my main concern. No one had a right to enter the school or classroom unannounced, and create havoc like this parent did. I believed that if I remained calm the mother would eventually wear down so that we could talk. I stood by the reading table and watched her throw books off the desks. She walked around the room and yelled, "No one knows what I've been through!"

She looked at me, tore her blouse in front, and showed me visible knife scars on her chest. "My ol' man did this to me!" She was sobbing when she approached me. She put her head on my shoulder and bawled. Then she turned and paced around the room. It was obvious to me she was on some kind of substance. I continued being calm while watching her every move. (I knew this mother well. She was always nice to me)

One of the students barely opened the door and said, "Ms. Michaux, you need any help?" (Three boys stood out in the hall ready to come to my aid.)

"Get out of here and go home now!" I yelled.

The mother came over to the table, sat down, and said, " I need a smoke."

"Fine with me." I replied as I sat down beside her. At this stage, she could smoke if that calmed her down. When she opened her purse, an empty rum bottle fell on the floor.

"What am I going to do?" she wailed.

"You're going to sit here and talk to me," I said.

She started talking about why she was so upset. Then, the door burst open! Two burley security officers ran into the room and grabbed her. The mother resisted and started screaming. The security officers tried to handcuff her. She slugged the closest one to her and escaped into the hall. They caught her and she was handcuffed. She was yelling obscenities as they escorted her down the hall.

Unfortunately, the parent's daughter was in the counselor's office. She heard her mother screaming and ran into the hall. The child started screaming and kicking the officers. I grabbed the daughter and put her in a safety hold as she cried and screamed for her mother. The mother was arrested. The father picked up his distraught daughter later.

After work that day, I stopped by the teacher's home to see how she was. She was still shaken by the incident. She thanked me for taking the time to stop by.

All of the doors were locked the next day. A doorbell and intercom system were installed. The mother made bail and came by the school a week later to apologize for her behavior. We talked for a while and then she left.

Two weeks later, I was summoned to court over the incident at school. The judge called the mother and me to the stand. He told the mother to apologize to me.

"I've already apologized to Ms. Michaux," she said.

He said, "You will publicly apologize to her in front of the court."

She looked at me and said, "Ms. Michaux, I'm sorry for what I did at the school." With that said, she put her arms around me and kissed me on the cheek! Everyone in the courtroom laughed! I did, too.

* * *

When the morning bell rang for students to go to their classrooms, a sixth grader ran into the office and yelled, "Ms. Michaux come quick! (There were no classroom phones)

I hurried with the student down the hall to the back stairwell. A sixth grade teacher stood between a parent and a sixth grade student. The teacher was mediating a heated argument between the mom and student. I told all three to come up into the hall, and told the parent to stand beside me. I told the scared student to stand by the teacher.

I said to the teacher, "Thanks for your help. Everyone be quiet. What happened?"

The teacher said, "This mother is upset because my student spent the night with her daughter on Friday night. On Monday, when my student came to class, she told everyone that the daughter wet the bed, and that she had pee on her pajamas. Some of the students made fun of her daughter at school. Now, she doesn't want to come to school anymore. This morning, the parent got into the school, came up the back stairwell, and grabbed my student. I heard them screaming at each other in the stairwell."

I took the parent with me and dismissed the teacher and student to class. The mother made several negative remarks under her breath as I escorted her to the office. I went into my office and called security to come at once. I asked the parent to tell me her side of the story. She repeated what the teacher had said while adding a few curse words.

Security arrived shortly, and I explained, "This parent came into Johnson School illegally and threatened one of my students and the teacher. Please explain the law to her." A written statement was taken and I filed charges against her. The parent got upset when she realized how serious the charges were. I said, " No one has a right to enter Johnson School for the purpose of threatening students and staff."

The parent was escorted out of the building by the security officer while the other officer took the teacher's and my statement. The parent was banned from the school property. The officers visited the home of the student who was threatened and told her mother about the incident. The banned parent moved out of our school district the next week.

* * *

An irate parent, big burly Mr. Smoot, stomped into the front office and demanded to see me. I ushered him into my office and sat behind my desk. I usually sat at the round table with a parent, but today I was leery of Mr. Smoot's behavior. He remained standing, shaking his index finger at me, and said, "What gives you the right to suspend Shawn from the bus? He was defending himself when he slugged the boy for spitting in his face!"

I said calmly, "Mr. Smoot, there are bus rules; a student will be suspended for fighting on the bus. The driver had to stop the bus. The bus monitor had each boy sit in the front seats away from each other. Your son, Shawn, chose not to listen, and continued punching the student in the face. The bus driver radioed for assistance. The bus for problem students was sent to pick Shawn up. I know you had to drive to the bus garage to pick him up, but your son chose to be disrespectful to the bus driver and monitor by continuing to fight."

"You listen to me. What happened to my son was wrong. No kid is going to spit in my son's face and get away with it. You had no right to suspend him from the bus for a week. I'm gonna' tell on you. I'm gonna' tell the superintendent what you did and have you fired. You can't treat my son this way!" he yelled, as he was pacing back and forth in my office, shaking his index finger at me.

I sat quietly behind my desk while he ranted and raved. He worked himself into a "big mad" and needed to vent. There was nothing I could say that he wanted to hear. Finally, he stopped pacing, looked at me and said, "Why aren't you upset?"

I looked him in the eyes, and replied, "You're upset enough for both of us, so you vent, and I'll stay calm."

Mr. Smoot sat down then, his anger turning to frustration. I said, "Why are you really upset?" He looked at me and said, "I have to be at work by 7:00a.m.and have no way to get Shawn to school. I can pick him up in the afternoon but I can't bring him in the morning."

"Mr. Smoot, Ms. Parton lives three doors down from you. She drives her children to school every morning. Why not ask her to bring Shawn to school, too? The Hayden family lives one street over. They drive their child to school on their way to work. They may be able to help also," I said.

Mr. Smoot stood up, thanked me for the information, apologized for his behavior, and left. I walked into the main office after he left the school. One of the office employees said, "We were going to call security if he continued yelling. But things got real quiet in there. Is everything O.K.?"

"Yes," I replied, and got a much needed cup of coffee.

* * *

One parent at Johnson felt school rules didn't apply to her. At breakfast time in the cafeteria, the parent sneaked past the breakfast monitor. She walked into her daughter's classroom un-announced to talk to the teacher. (Board policy stated all visitors had to register in the office before going anywhere in the building.)

When the bell rang for students to go to classes, the parent continued to talk to the teacher even as she greeted the students. The teacher told the parent to please leave so she could start class. The parent refused and continued talking.

One of the staff members saw the parent in the classroom and told me about it. I went to the room, told the parent that the teacher had to teach class, and that she had to leave. "If you want to schedule a conference with the teacher, please come to the office, and we'll arrange a time," I said.

The parent became belligerent with me. She said, "I have a right to talk to my child's teacher."

"You're exactly right," I replied, "But not now. The teacher has a right to teach, and students have a right to learn. You are interfering with the process." (Why did some parents feel they were above the law?)"You can walk out of here peacefully or be escorted by security."

"You Bitch!" she yelled at me, as she walked out of the classroom. There were a few other negative words she also said as she exited the school building. I called security and they made a home visit. They informed her that she was banned from the school building because of her behavior. She waited outside for her daughter at the end of the school day. They moved the next week.

I supported my staff when there was an unsafe situation at school. Teachers had to feel safe in the workplace.

* * *

There were times I wanted security to be stationed in our school to take care of violent parents. An upset mother came into my office to talk about an incident that happened to her daughter (our student) over the week-end. I left the door ajar as she sat down at the round table.

"Over the week-end, my daughter and Missy, another student, got into a fight. They were pulling hair and scratching each other real good. Be damned if Missy's grandmother got in the fight, too, with her cussin' and yellin' at my daughter. Then I got in a fight with the grandmother."

About that time my office door opened. In walked Missy's grandmother. She yelled, "I knew that Bitch would come up here and tell you lies about me!"

I jumped up, got in her face, and she stepped backwards. "You cannot come into my office without being invited. You calm down, now!"

No sooner had the words come out of my mouth, when the seated mother, jumped up behind me, pointed her finger over my shoulder to the grandmother, and yelled, "You Bitch, I knew you'd come here, and start trouble!"

The scene changed. We were in the main office now. The grandmother in front of me pulled out a kitchen knife while screaming at the mother behind me. She waved it high in front of me while trying to cut the mother behind me. The mother behind me yelled, "Just try to cut me, Bitch!"

I yelled, "Stop! Or I'll have both of you arrested!"

There was no sign of anyone in the office. A few people were hiding under the desks not knowing what happened.

"Millie (grand mother), put the knife away and leave the building now! "I yelled. Thank God she backed off and left while mumbling a few obscenities under her breath. I told the mother behind me to sit down while I called Security. "Why?" she whined. "I didn't do nothin' wrong."

The mother sat there until security came which was in record time. They took her side of the story, then visited Missy's home, and banned her grandmother from the school. Later, she called and apologized for bringing a kitchen knife to school.

* * *

One day, a student in the one of the Special Education classes was out of his medication. I called his mother and ask her to bring his medication to school.

Thirty minutes later, the mother walked into the office, wearing a white halter top, cut-off jean shorts, and flip flops. She was well endowed in the chest and had a long stemmed rose tattooed into her cleavage. When she spoke, she used exaggerated arm gestures and facial expressions. Her rose swayed while the office workers stared.

"Here's Peter's medicine. I told him to take it this morning but he forgot again. I'm gonna' have the 'ol man bust his butt when he gets home from school," she said.

I swear that I saw the rose grow an inch while she was talking! When the mother left, I told the office workers, "When I retire, I'm going to get a rose tattoo. Mine will look wilted compared to hers!"

* * *

There were many times, during my first year as a principal, that I was overcome by the huge responsibility of being Johnson's instructional leader. Some days at 6:30 p.m., when heading home to the south end of town, I questioned why I was chosen to be the principal of Johnson Elementary.

As the new principal, I soon realized two things; staff morale was low, and teachers had concerns about my leadership. There were some teachers at Johnson who felt "burned out." They interviewed every year to be transferred to a suburban school.

I came to school positive, energetic, and ready to be the best that I could be. Some of the staff wondered if I would survive the year. Others felt I had a "Pollyana" outlook on educating inner city students.

One day a teacher saw me hug a student in the hall. "You'd better not hug the students; you'll get your clothes dirty," she said.

16

"I need the hugs; I can always clean my clothes." I replied

"Surely you don't think these kids will amount to anything do you?" she asked. I was appalled. The teacher transferred at the end of the year.

* * *

The first year was a constant challenge for me. However, learning to overcome the challenges would prove invaluable in the years to come. I made so many mistakes along the way.

For instance, I assumed the Basal Reading Program approach was the right one for our students since it had been used at Johnson for several years, in first-sixth grades. During the first few months of school, I was in the classrooms observing the curriculum being taught. There were three levels of reading groups in every classroom. Workbooks or ditto copies were used when students were at their desks, before, or after their reading group lesson with the teacher. All students knew who was in the top reading group and who was in the low reading group. There were several non-readers in every primary class. (Primary was first grade through third grade. Kindergarten was half day in the 1980's.)

"Round Robin" was very popular. The reading group sat in a circle in chairs or on the floor with the teacher sitting in a chair. The students took turns reading a paragraph, page, or pages from their reading book. The goal of the teacher was to get through the reading book by the end of the year. Some students had two books to finish by the end of the school year.

I didn't understand why most of our students were having difficulty reading. Obviously the Basal Reading Program alone did not work. I wondered what other reading programs could be incorporated into the curriculum to help our students read?

I had the same concern with math. The math books were too difficult for many of our students to read and understand. Fee money was limited so the workbooks to go with the math books were not purchased. Teachers had to create their own math worksheets and run them off on the ditto machine. However, some of the ditto sheets were faded and the students couldn't read them. The teacher then, put the problems on the board which took up valuable time. Thank goodness the copier machine came several years later.

When students had difficulty reading in the Basal Reading Program, they went to another classroom with a Chapter I teacher who was funded by the federal government. (Later called Title I.) Reading skills were practiced. The non-readers went to the Remediation teacher for intense reading skills instruction funded by the state government.

Students with learning disabilities or difficulties in class were observed by their teachers in the areas of reading, math, writing and behavior. Weekly tests and behavior charts in reading, math, and writing samples, documented areas of concern. The teacher then worked with the student individually for weeks, re-teaching the skills when necessary. If the student showed little or no improvement, a Special Education Facilitator observed the student and wrote recommendations for improvement. If the Facilitator recommended that the student be tested for Special Education Services, the parents were notified by letter. A school had to have parent permission, in writing, to test their child for Special Education.

Once the student was tested for Special Education, an ARC (Admission and Release Committee) meeting was held. The group discussed the test results. Observations made by the teacher and Facilitator determined the educational program that was best for the student. The parent/guardian had to be present, along with the teacher, principal, Facilitator, Resource Room teacher, and any person the parent wanted in attendance. (Lawyer, advocate, relative, or friend.)

Through consensus of the committee, if the student needed special services in the areas of concern in a Resource Room, an I.E.P. (Individual Educational Program) was written for the student. The IEP dictated how many hours a week the student would spend in the Resource Room with the Special Education Teacher. The parent received copies of the minutes which included the child's IEP from the meeting.

* * *

I observed what was working in the curriculum and what wasn't. I didn't make any changes in the curriculum during the first semester. The staff was tolerant of my leadership style to a degree. Some wondered if a physical education teacher could be an instructional leader and rightly so.

There were times when I spent hours on the phone after school, and on week-ends, talking to other new principals and the former Johnson principal.

The new principals were overwhelmed at the responsibilities involved with the job, especially leaders with schools similar to Johnson. In the evenings, I listened to motivational tapes and CDs hoping to gain insight into my leadership role. I discovered Dr. Wayne Dyer who has inspired, motivated, and made me laugh at his candid sense of humor, wit, and wisdom. He helped me through some very difficult times in my professional and personal life.

* * *

As I mulled over the curriculum and thought about how we might help our students progress, I realized that I needed a well trained staff. I firmly believed that the teachers knew what training they needed to improve their teaching strategies, although several chose to observe other teachers first. Some of the teachers observed master teachers, teaching reading and math programs at other schools in the county. Central Office gave us permission to have substitutes for these teachers for one day.

At a staff meeting following the observations, teachers discussed the different reading and math programs they had seen. Perhaps, these reading and math programs would be suitable for some of our students.

A few of the teachers who had been teaching many years didn't agree with any new training. They had taught the same curriculum for a long time and felt that it worked. Some believed new and different approaches to the curriculum were not necessary.

All year, I observed teaching strategies in the classrooms. During my observations, I documented effective/ineffective teaching (according to our teacher evaluation form). Some teachers had effective teaching strategies for the students. It was a joy to observe them. Some teachers gave a lot of "busy work" instead of actually teaching the class. One teacher kept no plan book.

"How do I know what is being taught if it isn't in the plan book?" I asked.

"I put it on the board every morning," she replied.

"Not if you're sick and not here. You must keep a plan book so a substitute teacher will know what to teach if you are absent. I need to know what you are teaching the students also," I said.

She and I had a meeting with the area superintendent and he echoed my demand, "You must keep a plan book." She retired at the end of the year.

* * *

There were sessions with all of the teachers to improve their teaching strategies, and/or classroom management. Most improved, but there were a few teachers who went behind closed doors in the classroom and taught the same way they had for many years.

Fayette County's teacher evaluation form focused on ten areas to be observed and evaluated. The teachers were given a copy of the evaluation form at the beginning of the year and it was discussed in staff meeting.

Before observations began, I told the teachers about the areas being observed. Since I was in the classrooms throughout the school year, the teachers and I worked on any improvements needed before the evaluation started. Three or more observations were documented for each teacher being evaluated.

I supported teachers who transferred to schools in the suburbs. Granted, I lost some good teachers, but I felt it was a good thing when teachers transferred. I needed people on staff who believed in my philosophy (that all students could excel academically), and who really wanted to teach in the inner city at Johnson School. Some of the staff stayed with me for sixteen years while others, who were good teachers, needed a change, and transferred.

* * *

One teacher came to see me and shared her frustration. "I don't enjoy teaching here with all the social issues my students have. How can I be a good teacher when half of my students move each semester? The new students who come into my class in the middle of the year are more needy than the students who left," the teacher lamented. She transferred to an upper middle class school the following year. She told me that she was happy because her students stayed with her all year.

* * *

One important thing I learned as a principal was that in order to implement a new program you believed would benefit the students, you had to have support and "buy-in" from your staff. They have to be involved with every aspect of the program from the training to implementation and documentation. Otherwise, it dies on the paper where it was written. It doesn't matter if you think it will work. If your staff doesn't believe in it, it's just window dressing.

The Johnson staff was dedicated to improving our students' reading and math scores. Johnson students who stayed with us through their elementary years received a solid foundation in education.

* * *

The computer lab was installed in the late 1980's. It really impacted student interest in the curriculum. Students learned word processing and how to use the internet. They became proficient in many educational computer programs. Several of our Special Education students and self-contained Special Education students (students stayed with the same teacher all day), excelled in computer literacy. All students were tested on the computer in reading and math each year. Some of our students who didn't write well found the computer to be a teaching tool for improved writing skills. Due to ARC decisions over the years, some of the students in Special Education had a personal lap top which they used in all classes.

Johnson School was honored to be one of two elementary schools in the nation to have a "Take Home Computer Program." In 1989, ten families received a home computer and were trained on its various programs. The student and parent had computer homework every night. The next morning, the student returned the "floppy disk" to the lab assistant to have the homework checked. At the end of six weeks, ten new families received computers to use at their homes. Our families really appreciated the program because it was the only way they had an opportunity to become computer literate. Their children taught them how to use the computer, working with fifty parents who were happy to learn. Unfortunately, the next year, the program was not implemented due to lack of funds. The parents, staff, students, and I were all very disappointed.

* * *

Housing three primary self-contained classrooms at Johnson was both a blessing and a challenge. Self- contained primary was six to eight year olds. After sixth grade students went to middle school, primary was five to seven year olds. The Special Education students in the three classrooms taught us patience and a broad understanding of the challenges that special needs children faced. We, the staff, learned more about cultural diversity and relationships from these classes than any previous training had offered.

The three primary self-contained classes were EBD (Emotionally/Behaviorally/Disturbed) students, EMH (Emotionally/Mentally Handicapped) students, and SPH (Severely/Profoundly Handicapped) students.

Through ARC meetings, students from other schools in the county

21

were placed in the self-contained classrooms at Johnson. Some of our students were also placed there. Through the years, the majority of self-contained students came from other schools. Each student had an IEP with written goals and objectives to be achieved during the school year.

In a self-contained primary classroom, the teacher and assistant stayed with the students all day. They monitored each student's IEP in the classroom and other areas outside the classroom. They had breakfast, lunch and recess together. All three primary self-contained classrooms were highly structured with the same schedule everyday. It was important that the students knew what the daily classroom school day entailed. If there were changes in their daily schedule, the students had to be prepared ahead of time. Parents received daily/weekly progress reports from the teacher which were to be read, signed, and returned to school the next day.

In the EBD class, several students had physical outbursts at times during the school year. These outbursts resulted in chairs being thrown, other students being grabbed or hit, and partial destruction of the classroom. This occurred before the teacher or assistant could address the negative behavior. A buzzer in their classroom was connected to the principal's office. When it sounded, I ran to the room to remove the student who was out of control. Sometimes, the assistant walked the "behavior problem student" to my office. Other times, the student had to be carried from the classroom, while kicking and screaming, to the office, by staff who were trained in Safe Physical Management.

An EBD student came to my office only after time-outs in class, redirection, and behavior charts were used during class activities. However, physical outbursts in which the student or others in class could be hurt warranted immediate removal from the class to my office. The student was sent to the S.A.F.E. room to work after he calmed down.

In some cases, the student's erratic behavior escalated and school security was called to escort the student home. When a student had to go home, either the assistant or I rode with the security officer. The student sat in the back seat of the car. Sometimes, the parent/guardian picked up the unruly student at school, but usually, the student went home in a security car. Some of the more aggressive students, who were in the back seat of the car, kicked and punched at the metal grate separating the back seat from the front. They screamed obscenities and threatened to kill all of us. Sometimes, the waiting parent/guardian needed assistance getting the student from the car to the house. Most of the time, the student became quiet when the parent/foster parent was seen.

Several of Johnson School EBD students took medication. Some students had personal assistants who stayed with them all day. (If an ARC determined that a student needed a personal assistant, one was requested.)

One year, a student from another school, a "biter," was transferred to our EBD unit by way of an ARC meeting. The teacher, assistant, counselor, and I, who worked closely with the student, had to get a series of Hepatitus-B shots from the local health department. The student did not attempt to bite anybody at Johnson.

An effective program for children with severe behavior problems was a residential school called Re-Ed. (Rehabilitation Education). It was located near Eastern State Hospital in Lexington. The students lived on-site with counselors, therapists, and other staff members. The students learned coping skills for anger issues. They also learned how to change their way of thinking by reacting to their problems in a non-violent way. Parents were required to attend weekly therapy sessions with the student to learn how to interact with their child at home. The students in our EBD self-contained classroom, who came from Re-Ed, had improved behavior. As a follow through, one of the Re-Ed counselors ate lunch, weekly with the student. It was a very effective program.

EBD students with improved behavior, and improved classwork, were allowed to visit peers in the regular classroom for lunch, recess, or special classes.(Art, Music, Physical Education, or Library.) The classroom assistant stayed with the student. When the student's behavior continued to improve, the student stayed in the regular classroom for most of the day. (The ARC determined how long a student stayed in the regular classroom after meeting IEP goals and objectives.) The EBD self-contained unit was designed to improve students' behavior so they could return to the regular classroom. Structure and consistency at school and at home were vital components for a successful program.

EBD students who lived out of the Johnson School area, who improved enough to go to a regular classroom in their school district, chose to stay at Johnson the following school year. The teacher and the assistant did an outstanding job teaching life skills, behavior modification, and academic skills to every student in their class each year.

* * *

One of Johnson School's self-contained classes was the SPH. (Severely/Profoundly Handicapped). The teacher and assistant were trained in teaching and in working with non-verbal, handicapped students. Some of the students who were in wheelchairs and diapers, and were unable to speak, or feed themselves, had a personal assistant. A few students were toilet trained but couldn't speak or sign. Several students had been in foster care since birth. Only five students were in the class do to the intensity of their special needs.

Several of the students learned to sign with their hands. Others made gutteral noises or used pictures for learning. Picture teaching and sounds were used in practicing vocabulary and word recognition everyday.

Physical Therapy and Speech Class were part of the SPH learning process. ARC meetings determined how often each student received services. Speech services were available to all Johnson students who needed them.

During the school year, one of the students, Harvey, learned to walk to the office for his teacher's mail. He, then, was able to return to the classroom unassisted. I commended the teacher and assistant for their dedication to the students each year. Every student improved in life skills and academic skills under their guidance.

* * *

The third self-contained unit at Johnson was the EMH (Educably/Mentally Handicapped). Students were placed in this unit through an ARC meeting at their home school. Performance tests, low I.Q. (Intelligence Quotient), behavior, and other data collected, as well as other disabilities, determined the student's placement.

The teacher and assistant in the EMH classroom were very effective in teaching social skills along with reading and math. It was a joy to observe their classroom because of their creativity and positive teaching. Some of the students improved enough to spend part of their day in the Resource Room. Many students' behavior improved as well as their basic skills in reading and math.

I pay tribute to all three teachers and assistants for their passion and dedication to their students. I was proud to be their principal.

* * *

Students in the self-contained units were bussed to and from Johnson everyday. A teacher or assistant greeted them as they got off the bus in the morning and escorted them back to the bus in the afternoon. Some students wore special harnesses to secure them to their seats.

* * *

A regular school bus brought students to Johnson School who lived a mile or more away. Those who lived within a mile of the school had to walk. However, due to the fact that there was no sidewalk by the African Cemetery #2, on Seventh Street, the students who lived within a mile, on the cemetery side, rode a bus.

Sometimes, there were a few car riders, but not on a consistent basis. At dismissal, bus riders were called first, then car riders, then walkers. A certified teacher was on duty for the regular bus each morning and afternoon. All special area teachers (Physical Education, Music, Art, Library, etc.) without homerooms had bus duty.

* * *

Having been a physical education teacher for eighteen years before becoming the principal of Johnson School, provided me the opportunity to be on bus duty in the mornings or afternoons. I remember a funny incident which occurred one morning on bus duty while I was at Meadowthorpe Elementary School. It was 7:15 a.m. An irate parent was dragging her third grader to the entrance of the school yelling, "He's done two hundred and fifty farts and he's not doin' anymore!"

Dumbfounded, I agreed, and showed her to the principal's office. Later in the morning, the principal told me that the day before, the student had gone into the classroom, after recess, making "farting" sounds under his armpits. The class roared with laughter. The teacher told him to stop but the student continued to make armpit noises.

"For your homework tonight, you will write fart five hundred times and turn it in to me before class, tomorrow." The teacher said.

The principal agreed with the parent that writing two hundred and fifty farts were enough to write. When the parent left, the teacher was reprimanded for excessive punishment of a third grader. I do not believe that writing lines for bad behavior is effective.

* * *

When I had early morning bus duty at Julius Marks Elementary School, years later, I walked into the office at 7:00 a.m. and heard the phone ring. The principal answered, "Good morning, Julius Marks School."

A voice said, "Ben Boyle is sick and won't be at school today."

The principal replied, "Who am I talking to?"

The voice replied, "My daddy."

The principal yelled, "Ben Boyle, you better get to school right now or I'm coming to get you!"

When Ben finally came to school that morning, I said, "Ben, the next time you try to skip school, write down what you're going to say before you make the call." He looked at me red faced and went to class.

* * *

When I became principal of Johnson School, I believed that all of the previous years of teaching had groomed me for the position. I had to have a sense of humor in the leadership role to keep my sanity. I liked to hear funny stories and jokes. I also told a few myself.

I learned to laugh instead of dwelling on all the mistakes I made. Hopefully, I learned from them so they that were not repeated. Laughter helped sustain me through the rough times and kept balance in my life.

* * *

In the 1980's paddling was allowed in the schools. There were a few times, with parental permission, and a witness, that I paddled a student. One parent wanted to come to school and "bust his butt" (her son) over his negative behavior in class. I said, "No, that isn't allowed. You can discipline him at home. He 's going to S.A.F.E. to do his work." Eventually, paddling was eliminated by the school board and the paddle disappeared from my office.

* * *

One January, in the mid 1980's, Johnson School had a fifty-two percent turnover of students. Some of the teachers' record books had the names of half of their classes marked out and new names listed at the bottom of the page. One teacher had so many students withdraw and move from November to December, that she needed another record book in January to add new names. In a monthly assembly I pleaded with the students to stay at Johnson all year. The P.T.A. even had an evening meeting advising the parents not move until the end of the year. I asked parents to tell us if they were moving but few did. We had to count them absent until they enrolled elsewhere. This lapse affected our daily attendance, but as families were evicted or left before rent was due, new families moved in.

* * *

With a transient population in the community, supplies had to be on hand for the new students who enrolled each month without any supplies. Most needed clothing and several came with head lice issues. I called the minister of Southland Christian Church, with a congregation of six thousand members, and asked for his assistance. His youth minister had a great idea to help our students.

For an outreach service program one month, each Southland Christian Sunday School child brought a box of crayons, scissors, glue, or paper to the church. These were donated to Johnson School students. The youth minister brought enough supplies for one hundred new students who would enroll throughout the school year, as well as extra supplies for each classroom. Another week of the month, the Sunday School classes brought in tissues, band aids, and bars of soap that were delivered to the school.

Teachers had "community" scissors, pencils, crayons, and glue in baskets on each table in the primary classes. Stealing was no longer an issue because the supplies belonged to everyone. If a child brought in a box of crayons, they were added to the community basket.

Some of our parents who bought their children supplies had a hard time with the concept of "community sharing, " in the beginning. However, they soon saw that it benefited their child in the long run.

One time, all Southland Sunday School children donated gently used winter coats. When the coats were delivered to the school, they were available to our children, and were worn home the same day. Thank you, Southland Christian Church.

* * *

Johnson School Average Daily Attendance (ADA) determined the amount of funding the state awarded the school. In the early years of my leadership, attendance was a concern. If the students came to school they would learn, but it was difficult to get the children to school everyday. Students missed school for many reasons including no clothes to wear, no alarm clocks in the home, head lice, or students babysitting younger siblings so the parent could run errands.

Often, a few Johnson School families moved when the rent was due or they faced eviction. The students were counted absent at school until they enrolled at another school. School attendance suffered during these times because it could be two to three weeks before the students enrolled at another school, especially if they moved out of county or out of state.

One parent really frustrated me. She had four children who missed several days of school each month. She got tired of the truancy letters which were sent home each week. So she withdrew all four from Johnson School to "home school" them.

The parent provided a letter from the director of attendance stating she was "home schooling" her children. A day later, people in the community called me complaining about her children being out of school vandalizing property. I told them to call the police.

I called the truancy officer to ask him to visit the home to make sure the children were being taught academics everyday. He did. When he saw no children having school at the house, he said to the mother, "Where are the children?"

The mother smirked and replied, " My kids go to night school."

I was very upset about the incident because I knew the children were not being educated. However, parents had a legal right to "home school" their children. Several students in the county who were "home schooled" were being taught by educated, caring parents. In my opinion, this parent denied her children an education to avoid going to court for truancy.

* * *

One of the fourth grade honor students was habitually tardy. It was the second month of my first year as principal. Johnson started at 8:55 a.m. At 9:15 a.m., Mrs. Walters and Evonna came into the office.

"Ms. Michaux, I know we're late, again, but I couldn't find Evonna's pink beads for her hair, and she wouldn't come to school without them."

"Mrs. Walters, Evonna is one of our top academic students in the fourth grade. Being tardy every morning has caused her to miss the teacher's morning instructions, again. She's missing valuable instructional time; seventeen tardies are too many. Please get Evonna to school on time," I said.

Mrs. Walters turned around and walked out the front door.

At my wit's end, I called the truancy officer for our school, a beautiful African American lady who formerly taught at the original Dunbar High School, downtown. Afterward, she went to work at Central Office.

She knew many of the black families whose children attended Johnson School.

I said, "Ms. Mooney, I need your help. Will you make a home visit with me to a black family's home to discuss excessive tardies? I have talked with the mother several times about this, and have written notes home. The mother gets Evonna to school on time for a few days and then the tardies begin again. Perhaps it's a cultural thing since I am the first white, female principal at Johnson, since Ms. Lovely in 1939. I'd like you to make the home visit with me. I'll "shadow" you and observe the way you converse with Mrs. Walters."

Dead silence on the phone. Then Ms. Mooney said, "Ms. Michaux, this is the strangest request I've ever had from a principal. Sure, I'll do it."

The following afternoon Ms. Mooney and I visited Mrs. Walter's home. After introductions, we were seated in the living room. Ms. Mooney said, "Mrs. Walters, Kentucky law states that all students must attend school, on time, everyday. Evonna has seventeen tardies."

"I know. Ms. Michaux told me," she replied.

"Legal action will be taken if Evonna continues to be late for school," Ms. Mooney said.

"She told me that, too." she replied. (I thought, so far so good.)

Then Ms. Mooney squinted her eyes and said, "Mrs. Walters, are you a Christian?" (Aha, I thought, black people talk about religion.)

"Why, yes I am," said Mrs. Walters.

Not wanting to be left out, I exclaimed, "That's wonderful! I'm a Christian, too."

Ms. Mooney looked at me and said, Ms. Michaux, Mrs. Walter's maiden name was "Christian" before she married Mr. Walters."

Both women heehawed, slapping their hands on their knees in riotous laughter. I could have crawled under the coffee table! Then I laughed, too. Mrs. Walters slapped me on the back and said, "Ms. Michaux, you're O.K."

When Ms. Mooney and I returned to her car, she asked, "Ms. Michaux, do you see any cultural differences now between you and the black families?"

Meekly, I replied, "No."

She laughed all the way back to Johnson School. Evonna came to school on time for the rest of the year.

Head lice caused many absences. When it came to lice control, I feel that we set the parents up to fail. Johnson School's nurse came two half days a week. Most of her time was spent checking heads for lice, nits, or live bugs. If two or more students in the same class had lice, she had to check everyone's head in the class. It took up a lot of her time at school. If lice were found, the student was sent home. A letter was given to the parents from the health department stating that the child had lice and could not return to school until the child was "nit free."

The letter instructed the parent to go to the health department, pick up lice shampoo, treat everyone's head in the family, wash the sheets and clothing of the infected people, pick the live bugs and nits from the child's head, and return the child to school in three to five days. If there were too many nits in the hair at school, either I or the guidance counselor took the child home. If the child still had nits, the parent could return to the health department to receive more lice shampoo, and repeat the process.

In reality, the above process didn't happen. Most of our parents didn't have a car. If a friend drove them to the health department, a few miles away, they had to pay for the gas. If the parent walked, all the siblings had to walk, too.

Many of the children and parents didn't sleep on sheets. Some of the children slept on mattresses with no sheets, only blankets. Others slept on couches, chairs, and the floor. I knew this to be true from home visits where I saw the sleeping areas. Lighting in the house had to be good to pick nits. Some of the rental and Section Eight houses had one single light bulb hanging from the ceiling. This made seeing nits very difficult. This problem was frustrating to the parents and the children. They needed help.

One parent was so upset that her daughter had repeated head lice, that she rubbed mayonnaise into her scalp and hair so that she could return to school. Another parent shaved her son's head.

An irate parent came to the office one morning because I had sent his child home again because of lice. "You need to line up every kid here in the school, strip 'em, and spray 'em down like they do at the jail. I swear you must be breedin' the damn bugs in the school. My kids didn't get lice 'til you came here. It's all your fault. I'll get the damn shampoo so I can use it on 'em to get 'em back here tomorrow. This time they'll stay. I've a good mind to shave their heads," he said. He didn't want to hear anything

I had to say. He was non-threatening to me; he just wanted to vent. If he had gotten violent, I would have called security.

Looking for a solution, I asked the staff if anyone would volunteer to be trained as "nit pickers." The nurse wasn't at school every morning to check the heads of students returning to school after being treated. There were too many students for me to check some mornings. Five employees volunteered and were trained. If a returning student had a few nits, we could pick the nits off of each hair follicle, and the student could return to class. If there were too many to pick, the student was sent home. (The parent usually stayed until the child's head was checked.)

Sometimes the "nit pickers," the school nurse, and I had to make home visits to show the parents how to pick the nits. It was especially hard to see nits in blonde hair. (Our black children did not get lice at Johnson School.)

One day, the nurse couldn't reach a parent who had two blonde headed children with nits and live bugs at school. "Where does your mother hang out during the day?" I asked the children. "At Al's Bar," the boy said. "We go there when school's out."

I walked both children the five hundred yards to the bar. I went in, told the bar owner who I was, and who I needed to see. The students' mother came outside. I told the mother about the lice.

"I can't see no lice in their heads," she said.

So, on the corner of Sixth Street and Limestone Street, in the bright sunshine, I showed the mother the nits in her children's heads and how to pick them. I even showed the children how to pick each other's head. When the mother told the bar owner she had to take her children to the grandmother's house which was two streets over, he said, " Fine." He looked at me and said, "Anytime you need help over there at the school, you come and get me. If you need ice or anything like that for activities, you let me know." Amazing community!

* * *

Three smart girls in the Bland family were in the top reading and math groups in their grade levels. Their attendance problem was chronic head lice. They missed several days of school every month. They'd return to school after their hair was washed with lice shampoo. Within two days, they had to be sent home again because there were still nits in their hair. The health department parent letter stated that the student's head had to be "nit free."

Frustrated, the school nurse asked me to accompany her on a visit to their home because the family had no phone. It may seem strange for a principal to make home visits, but there had already been home visits from the guidance counselor, social worker, and teachers, over lice concerns. However, the lice problem and absences continued. I said to the mother, "The girls have missed so much school over head lice that it has become a truancy issue. I want to work with you so that we don't have to go to court."

The nurse showed the mother and the girls how to pick nits and live bugs from their heads. She told the parent to shampoo Granny's hair and the boyfriend's hair since they also lived there. She explained to the mother that the sleeping areas needed cleaning as well as any couch or chair that served as a bed. The mother realized the seriousness of the continual absences. Everyone in the family worked together to be "nit free." The girls' attendance improved.

At the beginning of the next month, Ms. Bland got a job at a local restaurant. I chose never to tell anyone about her lice issues. I was glad that she had gotten a job.

* * *

Two students were absent due to constant re-occurring head lice. They lived with their grandmother on Seventh Street. The counselor, social worker, and nurse had visited the home on different occasions to talk with the grandmother about the lice problem. They gave her lice shampoo but the students continued to be infested with "live" bugs.

The school nurse came into my office one morning and said, "Will you go with me to visit Grandmother Mosley and her two grandsons after school today? They have missed too much school and aren't getting rid of the lice problem. I talked to grandmother on the phone. She sprained her ankle and can't walk."

I agreed to go with her on the visit. We were sitting in the kitchen with grandmother and her two grandsons when we saw that grandmother's head was also full of lice. One of the boy's heads had only a few nits while the other one had many. All three of them had washed their heads with the lice shampoo given to them. The nurse worked on the boy's head with the most nits. I finished the other one. Then I started picking grandmother's head while she was seated in a chair with her sprained ankle propped up on another chair.

While we were engaged in picking "nits," a cat walked in the kitchen, jumped up on the table, stepped across the table to the stove, and began eating food out of pan. Then he walked to the sink counter and ate food off the plates. I was surprised that no one told the cat to get down on the floor. I continued working on grandmother's head. When the boys' heads were clean, I told them to get the blankets and sheets off the beds to wash. I called their state social worker from the house and asked if she could help the grandmother wash the sheets. She agreed to come later that day. The boys returned to school the next day and stayed the rest of the week, nit free.

* * *

Helping the families with lice issues slightly improved the students' attendance. I felt, however, that if we could have lice shampoo available in the school, our parents wouldn't have to walk to the health department to get it. This easy access to shampoo would have a positive impact on our attendance.

After school and on week-ends, I visited several pharmacies in the city, asking for lice shampoo donations. I had a letter in hand thanking them for the lice shampoo donation if one or more bottles was donated to the school. What caring pharmacies- they gave me cases of lice shampoo! I knew I could have called or written them a letter, but personal appearances were far more powerful. We kept the lice shampoo in the nurse's station under lock and key. If any lice shampoo was given to a parent, the parent's name was recorded, along with the number of bottles they were given. The parents were advised to shampoo everyone's head once, pick the nits, and repeat the process seven days later, if the lice were still visible.

When parents found out they could come to the school for lice shampoo, they were elated. One mother told me that she was glad Johnson School cared about her child. Taking the time to find a solution to this ongoing problem was such a simple gesture on my part. I learned a valuable lesson that day. It was that people don't care what you know until they know you care. My school parents didn't care how I dressed, or what kind of car I drove, they cared about how I treated them and their children. What I saw as a solution to a problem, many parents saw as helping them get their children to school. I strongly believed in treating everyone with kindness and respect. I had an open door policy at the school. I believed that if I could be pro-active and deal with family issues up front, in a positive way, I wouldn't have to go to court over truancies and educational neglect later.

Truancy was a challenge when families moved often. One year, the majority of the new students who enrolled in January had already been to two different schools.

A behavior concern with a new fifth grade student sent him to the office. Since he was new to Johnson, I brought his cumulative folder to my office to see what school he attended before enrolling at Johnson. In the back of the folder, it listed all the schools he had attended since kindergarten. He had been with us one week.

"Sam, this is your cumulative folder. It follows you through your school years. It lists all the schools you've been to before Johnson," I said, as I showed him the list. "You've been to six different schools."

He looked it over and said, "Ms. Michaux, there are two schools missing here. I was at a school in Lexington by the big shopping center for a month, and in a school in Nicholasville for a week. Do they count?"

"Yes, they count. Do you remember when you were there?"

"No." he said.

We looked at all his papers and test scores in the cumulative folder to see if any were from the two missing schools. He had taken a fourth grade test and the school name was on the heading. I called the school to see if they had his enrollment and withdrawal dates. They did. I wrote them in his folder. The school he was in for a week had no record of him being there, so I also made a note of it. The problem with both schools was that the teacher or designated person didn't take time to update the cumulative folder before sending it to the receiving school.

We looked at his grades and I said, "Sam do you know you are above average in reading and math? You also did very well on the state test considering you were in so many schools last year."

"I didn't know that. Thanks a lot for telling me," he beamed. He was a model student the following three weeks before he withdrew and moved.

One teacher was having difficulty finding the home of one of her students, so I went with her the next day. We found out it was the wrong address. The following day, I followed the student home. The mother was shocked to see me with her son because they had moved out of our school area.

Mom started making excuses. I said, "Please don't. Tell me the truth when you move out of district; we have resources that can help you if you want your child to stay at Johnson, but don't lie to me about your address." She filled out the Out of District papers and thanked us for being concerned about her child.

* * *

Some of our families moved in with friends until they could afford the rent for their own place. This happened often in the housing projects on east Sixth Street. A family could "visit" another family for two weeks, then they had to move, or the family renting could lose their apartment. The children were often tardy or absent.

One of the new families who enrolled from another county had three children. When we called the previous school they had attended, we were informed that the children had missed twenty days of school and were a truancy problem. (It was the first of November.)

The mother talked to me in my office, "The kids need clothes and shoes to wear."

"We can get clothing and shoes for the children but they must come to school everyday. Do you need an alarm clock?"

"Yes we do," she said.

The children were in school everyday the first week, then the absences started.

The counselor and I made a home visit the following week since there was no phone. (They lived in the housing project at the end of East Sixth Street.)

I knocked on the door. A voice said, "Come in."

I walked into the apartment where two mattresses were on the floor. Mom, boyfriend Walt, and three kids were laying on them sharing two blankets.

Mom said, "I overslept. I'll get the kids up to the school in an hour."

I thanked her and left. The children arrived at school in time for lunch.

The students' attendance improved except for second grader, Charles. He showed up Monday morning with sores in and on his mouth. The nurse examined him and suspected the herpes virus. The mother later confirmed it," He has medicine for the sores when they get pus in them. I have to keep him home then 'cause he's contagious. They dry up in a week or two."

The mother cooperated with us and seemed to care for her children.

A week later, I drove Rachel, who had impetigo, home (no phone).

When the student walked through the front door of her house, her mother and Walt (same boyfriend with the other family) were laying on the couch. He was as surprised to see me as I was to see him. The mother thanked me for bringing her daughter home. It was the first of the month. I suspected Walt was a "welfare check chaser."

The following week, Rachel and one of the new students got into a fight over Walt at recess. Rachel said," Walt likes my mother better than he likes your mother." Charles' sister disagreed and hit Rachel in the face. When they spent time in S.A.F.E., at recess the next day, I asked both mothers to come to school to see me at 12:00 noon.

They came into the office and sat down. "Are you all aware that your children have been fighting over Walt on the playground?"

Both mothers said, "No." They looked at each other and realized Walt was seeing both of them.

"Is Walt worth all of the fighting that he has caused your children at school?" I asked.

Neither mother said a word; they looked down at the floor.

"I'd be willing to bet that he has taken money from both of you."

They both nodded yes.

"You all need to resolve this problem so that your children will stop fighting at school."

One mother said, "Don't worry about that anymore. I got a job in Cynthiana. Rachel and me are moving this week-end. She can have him."

"I don't want the S.O.B. either. We'll take care of the problem." Charles' mother said.

The mothers left the office amicably and the children stopped fighting at school.

* * *

Teachers made conference calls and sent notes home for teacher/parent conferences when there was no home phone. Parent/teacher conferences, which were held every nine weeks, were vital for parents' knowledge of their child's academic success. Open communication between home and school made successful students in school.

One day a classroom teacher said to me, "Would you make a home visit to a student's home and talk to the mother about coming in for a conference? I have written three notes to the parent about times to meet. I asked her to call me with a convenient time but she has not replied to any of the notes. The student needs help in reading and her mother and I need to discuss it."

"Yes, I can go after school." I said. (The teacher already had conferences scheduled after school or she would have gone with me.)

I visited the mother after school. She invited me into the living room.

I said, "The teacher needs to talk to you about your daughter's grades."

She said, "Well, no one from the school told me about it."

"The teacher has written three notes to you about conferences. You haven't returned any with the time you could meet."

The mother hung her head and meekly replied, "I can't read."

Stupid, insensitive me. The thought never entered my mind that some of our parents were nonreaders. It was a turning point. Clearly, our parents did care about their children's education and wanted to be involved.

"When can you come to the school for a conference?" I asked.

"Tomorrow, after school," she replied. I thanked her for her time and returned to the school. The next day she came for a conference with the teacher.

I realized that the school had to be a warm and inviting place for the parents. We needed to offer reading classes to our parents who were nonreaders.

* * *

Several home visits were made to Margaret Carter's home by the attendance clerk and the school social worker. They were concerned about the student's five absences. The mother was not co-operative with them until she saw me on the fourth visit.

"Where is Margaret?" I demanded.

The mother sighed and said, "I had to put her in Charter Ridge Hospital. She had another episode and clawed me real bad." Margaret was a frequent visitor at Charter Ridge Hospital for her severe emotional problems. Her medical card only covered ten days of treatment there. It was frustrating for everyone who was concerned about Margaret's welfare. Obviously, she needed long-term care. Her previous medication had side effects so the mother stopped giving it to her.

Before Margaret was released from Charter Ridge Hospital, her Special Education teacher from Johnson, her mother, and I met with some of the staff who had worked with her. We discussed academics, therapy, and Margaret's medication as she was being sent home.

I asked if the medication could be given at school instead of home since her mother was not willing to give her the medication everyday. It was approved.

The positive outcome to this story was that the state social worker assigned to Margaret was able to drive her to the Comprehensive Care Center for weekly therapy visits. Thus, she also made sure that Margaret received her daily medication. She improved in both her behavior and academic subjects.

* * *

Early one morning two plain -clothes police officers came to Johnson School. They asked if I recognized two students in several photos. The two boys in the photos were wearing disguises of black rimmed glasses with big noses and black mustaches which they had brought. The pictures showed the boys' faces before the disguises, then the disguised faces while stealing a woman's purse from her, in a downtown parking garage.

I was surprised because they were two brothers, seven and ten years old, who were Johnson students. Apparently, women's purses had been "snatched" over a two-month period in the parking structure. The victims told the police that two young boys grabbed their purses. The pictures came from the parking garage video tape.

The police officers spoke to each boy separately. They called the boys' mother at work. She met her sons and the officers at the police station. (She had recently received custody of her sons after being released from prison.) The students told the police that their thirteen year-old brother showed them how to steal women's purses. The family moved from the area the next week.

Anytime, the police or social services came to school to interview students, they were legally allowed to do so without the parent's consent. There were parents who threatened me over the years, for allowing "those people" to speak to their child/children before I called them. I told the parents that their permission was not needed for police and social services workers to interview their children at school. This was the law. I said, "Please call the school superintendent if you are unhappy."

* * *

In some instances there were no positive solutions to family problems. Grandparents raised Dina during her elementary years at Johnson. By Dina's fifth grade year, her grandparents were in their late seventies and in poor health. Grandmother was on a walker which meant that the grandfather had to walk from Seventh Street to Johnson School for parent/teacher conferences with Dina's teachers. Dina had behavior issues. She had an outburst in class where she yelled obscenities to other students and had to be removed. She continued this drama in the guidance counselor's office.

I asked the grandfather to came to school. While the grandfather and Dina were in my office, she was agitated, and very disrespectful to him. Grandfather's appearance was pitiful. He had greasy hair and a week old beard. The urine odor was strong on his stained pants. He looked at me with sad eyes and said, "My wife and I can't care for Dina no more. Her momma's comin' to take over."

Dina started bawling. "I don't want momma here with me. I hate her. She took my sister with her and left me when I was little. She doesn't want me. I won't live with her." I walked Dina to the S.A.F.E. room to do her class work and drove grandfather home.

During summer break, Dina's mother and sister came for grandmother's funeral, and placed grandfather in a nursing home. The mother and two daughters lived in the grandparent's house.

Two years later Dina had a daughter. Five years later her daughter enrolled at Johnson School. Her guardian was Dina's mother because Dina ran off with an older man who lived in Corbin, Kentucky. Sometimes, there were no positive solutions to family problems.

* * *

An eleven-year old sixth grader was sent to the office for being sick and vomiting in the classroom. "How long have you been vomiting?" I asked.

She said, "About four days."

"Have you seen a doctor yet?"

She said, "No, but mom said to come home if I puke again. I live on Second Street now. (out of our school attendance area.) Mom don't got a car. Can you take me home?"

I said, "Yes." Then I noticed a hickey on her neck. "Do you have a boyfriend?"

"Yes." She said. "How did you know?"

39

"How old is he?"

"Seventeen years old," she replied. I drove her home as there was no phone. She enrolled at her new school the following week. Seven months later she gave birth to a baby girl

* * *

First grader Ranessa was sent to the office for writing her name on the wall in the girls' bathroom. "Ranessa, tell me what happened in the bathroom," I asked.

"I used it." she said.

"It states on this behavior report that you wrote your name on the bathroom wall with a marker."

"Uh-uh. Somebody else must a' wrote it," she said, as she kept her head down and didn't give me eye contact.

"Nobody else knows how to spell the name Ranessa but you. Look at me." (she did.) "I'm going to place my hand over your heart because your heart always tells the truth." (I did.) Her eyes got real big. "I'm going to ask you again, did you write your name on the bathroom wall? Remember you must tell the truth."

"I did it! I did it! But I won't do it anymore!" she yelled.

"Thank you for being honest with me. I have a rag and cleaner you will use to wash your name off the wall." We went into the bathroom and she cleaned her name off the wall. Ranessa returned to class.

* * *

Jackson was a new student with Touretts Syndrome, according to his mother. In the third grade, he made noises in class, barked like a dog, and swirled spit around in his mouth which made slobber sounds. He licked classmates on their hands, arms, and faces when he got near them. He had little control over his actions. He was a constant disruption in class, halls, and the cafeteria.

Jackson told his teacher that he was on medication but there was no phone number for his mother. She had not mentioned any medication when he enrolled. He was often sent to the office for behavior problems. One of his angry classmates said, "If he licks me one more time, I'll kick him in the balls. I don't care if I get suspended."

"You'll do no such thing," I said.

Jackson went to the S.A.F.E. room to work while the counselor and I made a visit to his home. Jackson's mother answered the door in a stretch leopard skin leotard. Dramatic hand gestures swung in semi-circles as she welcomed us into the living room.

"Come in! Come in!" she exclaimed. We entered and sat down on the couch. She draped her body over the chaise lounge as I introduced the counselor and told her our concerns about Jackson. " Jackson's been to the doctor for new medicine. I don't have the money for it every month, so I give him a pill here and there." she said.

"If we bought his medicine, would you give us permission to give it to him at school everyday?" I asked.

"Sure girl! she exclaimed.

When Jackson was on daily medication, he stayed focused in class, kept his hands and feet to himself, and the noises and licking stopped. He played with classmates at recess and his reading improved. During the holiday vacation, Jackson moved to another county.

* * *

The first five years of my principalship at Johnson School had a profound effect on my relationships with the families. When students got sick at school with no phone at home, for example, the counselor and I scouted the neighborhood in my van looking for the parent.

We always found the parent by following a pointed finger from the back seat. Students didn't know the street names but the finger in the back pointed left, right, or we heard 'keep going." Lack of phones in the homes was a concern; however, a solution was found for some families on Seventh and Shropshire Streets. There was a pay phone near the market on Seventh Street that I used when I needed to get a message to nearby parents. (I got the pay phone number from one of the parents.) When I called the pay phone, someone always answered. I said, "This is Principal Michaux at Johnson School. Will you please tell Ms. Pierce (or some other parent) to come to school and pick up their sick child?"

The message was delivered. In ten to twenty minutes, the parent arrived at the school to pick up the child. It was effective networking!

* * *

Over the years, I learned where most parents "hung out," if they weren't at home. I found them at a friend's house, the local bar, or a nearby market. Being able to find them during an emergency was crucial

41

when it involved their child. One time, I contacted a mother at her work place which was a local laundry. I said, "Your child's sick with a high temperature and needs to go home."

The mother informed me, "That is your problem. I am at work, and can't leave."

I replied, " That's fine. I'll bring him to you."

I drove the sick child to the laundry. The mother was upset until she saw how sick her son was. She apologized and took him home.

* * *

The majority of home visits were very positive. I found the home environment very inviting with many family pictures on the walls and comfortable furniture. Families took pride in their homes. On a few home visits I encountered several television sets, video recorders, and chrome tire rims stacked in a corner in the living room. It looked like stolen property to me but I was only there for truancy concerns.

* * *

The guidance counselor and I made a home visit to get a parent's signature for his son's Special Education test. I parked the van on a one-way street near the house. We walked up the steps to the front porch. In the window of the front door there were gold letters which read, "Day Sleeper Night Creeper." I knocked on the glass door. (It was 11:00 a.m.) After a few minutes I knocked again. A good-looking tall black man opened the door in a short white terry cloth bathrobe. "Good morning Ladies!"

I immediately introduced the counselor and myself. I stated the reason for our visit. "Come in! I have the papers on the table here in the hall," he said.

We followed him into the hall; he bent over the small table to sign the papers, and his robe hiked up in the back. I heard a gasp behind me as I looked up at the wallpaper on the wall. He handed me the signed paper. I thanked him, and we left.

In the van, driving back to Johnson School, I laughed and said to the counselor, "I think you got flustered on the home visit."

She looked at me and replied, "No, you're the one who's flustered. We're driving the wrong way on this one way street."

* * *

The Johnson staff was pro-active supporting the families with clothing, school supplies, and food. The staff and their friends brought in alarm clocks and clothes during the school year also. Our attendance improved.

In the monthly newsletters sent home, the parents were asked to tell us when they were moving so that we could contact their new school. Most of our parents and students let us know when the move was taking place; others left in the middle of the night to avoid paying rent or being evicted. Granted, the few parents who had addictions, had problems getting their children to school everyday. However, most of our parents appreciated everything we did for their children.

Many civic and community organizations wanted to do service projects to help poor people. It took time to find them but they were "out there" and were willing to help our families. I believed that two of my responsibilities as a leader were finding solutions to problems and removing the barriers to learning.

* * *

Three consignment shops donated clothes to Johnson School if we picked them up at their stores. Thus, began monthly trips during which I picked up bags of clothes at two stores and brought them to the school. The custodian sometimes picked up clothes at one store which was on his way home. The next day, he took the bags of clothing to the school clothing center. Parent volunteers sorted the clothes for the children and families. (Some of these donations were adult clothes).

Many people in the community needed furniture, beds, tables, chairs, and appliances. Several organizations, friends, and visitors, donated a lot of furniture, beds, and other furnishings. Over the years, I found that the "barter " system worked with families. I made them an offer: "If your child comes to school everyday, on time, for a week, you can have a donated couch." (or whatever item the family needed). The approach worked.

Toward the end of each month, some children had little or no food to eat. They had to wait until the welfare check came in the mail on the first of the month. Some of the markets in the area allowed parents to charge food until the checks arrived. However, I thought the interest on the charges were too high. Parents would get their check cashed at the market, and the money owed on the charge was paid first, so many parents were already behind for the month.

Few families moving into our school area brought the bare essentials with them. They arrived with clothes on their back and little else. They had no pots or pans, much less dishes and silverware; there was no furniture, beds, or chairs.

The cafeteria manager complained about the loss of silverware in the cafeteria one day. "They must be throwing the silverware into the trash can." she said. A few days later, a new student wearing a coat at lunch, walked out of the cafeteria. Two forks fell out of his pocket. He was sent to the office. I asked him to remove his coat. He did. He had a four piece-place setting of silverware inside his pockets. "We don't have nothing to eat with at home." he said.

"Stealing is against the law. You and I are going to the cafeteria. You'll give the silverware back to the manager and apologize. I'll visit your parent and see what is needed at your home. Do not steal anything again." He agreed and apologized.

* * *

On one home visit, at the end of the month, I saw a potato that had been cut up and fried in a pan. This was to be dinner for a student and her brother. There was a local food donation center in the area but a family could only use it once a month. Out of dire need, we started a food bank at the school. The parent volunteers kept it organized. When a parent came in for help, several canned goods were given to them to use until their check came.

It reminded me of Abraham Maslow's Hierarchy of Needs "… in order to arrive at self actualization as a human being, basic needs must first be met… food, clothing, and shelter."

* * *

On a few home visits I discovered that the families did not have money to wash the children's clothes at the laundromat. Thus, the clothes stayed in a pile on the floor for weeks. In some cases, the children had outgrown the pile of dirty clothes by the time there was money to wash them. (Food stamps did not cover detergent). One of the outreach programs at Southland Christian Church donated boxes of detergent to Johnson School. It was a great service to our families. If a parent volunteered at school, the parent received a box of detergent.

A suburban family donated a washer and dryer to Johnson. If a parent volunteered at the school, she could wash a load of clothes. It was short lived because there was no way to vent the dryer inside the school building.

The washer and dryer went to one of our fortunate families who had a hook up for the appliances.

* * *

Home visits taught me to appreciate our families. During several visits, the parents talked to me about concerns over the heating bill being too high, fear of eviction, scarcity of food, and personal concerns. I detected feelings of hopelessness from some of the parents, especially the ones in the federal housing project, because so many didn't see a way to better their life.

This hopeless feeling was foreign to me. I grew up in federal government housing in West Virginia. My father was killed in WWII, in 1945. My mother worked for Union Carbide Chemical Company in South Charleston. My grandmother, Nannie, lived with us, cooked for us, and helped raise my two sisters and me. We always knew we were going to college because mother said so. All three of us earned degrees and worked during our adult life.

After eighteen years of marriage, I divorced. I had two sons at home. It was a very painful and sad time for all of us. Mother said, "While you're feeling sorry for yourself, why don't you go back to school?"

"Mom, I haven't been to college in twenty years," I whined.

"Just take one class," she insisted. Mother knew best.

At Eastern Kentucky University, I met people just like me, who were improving their lives in higher education. Several times I dragged my eleven and fifteen year old sons to campus with me. Sometimes "Mama" Back (their babysitter when they were little) sat with them while I attended class. Once the Master's degree in Elementary Education was completed, along with a Rank I in Administration, I knew I wanted to be a principal. (I already had a B.S. Degree in Physical Education).

In 1985, the Fayette County Board of Education had two elementary schools which needed principals. One was in the suburbs and one was in the inner city. I interviewed for both. I visited the sites and knew where the schools were located. A week later, the superintendent called and said, "Another school has a principal vacancy. It's Johnson Elementary School. I want you to be the new principal. Will you accept the position?"

I had no idea where Johnson was located but I knew I wanted to be a principal, so I enthusiastically said, "Yes!"

At Johnson School's first Open House, after welcoming all the parents to the school, I told the parents about my background, that I had grown

45

up in West Virginia, in a housing project, and how I arrived at Johnson as their principal. I said, "If you have your high school diploma or G.E.D. I'd like for you to apply for several positions here at the school. We need cafeteria workers, cafeteria monitors for lunch, teachers' assistants, S.A.F.E. assistants, and custodians. Don't worry if you don't have experience. We will train you."

Holding jobs at the school worked out for many of the school parents. Over the sixteen years I was principal, many parents/grandparents worked at the school, in all areas. Three went on to higher education and one became a teacher at Johnson School! I strongly believed that empowering people to improve their lives was key to finding their purpose in life. Clearly, hiring qualified parents and grandparents in the community had a positive impact inside the school. They excelled in the educational environment. Several worked at Johnson School for many years.

Neighborhood Scenes

Johnson Elementary School was located in a busy neighborhood. At all hours of the day people walked up and down the streets and through the alleyways beside and behind the school.

There were homeless people with grocery carts filled with all kinds of "stuff." Plastic bags hung from the sides. One man pushed a grocery cart with an aluminum door in it. The door even had hinges and screws. Noticing my stare, he told me that he was taking it to Baker's (Baker's Iron and Metal Company) which was a few blocks from the school, to get cash.

The police were visible on horseback, bicycles, and cars several times during the day. Dogs roamed freely on the playground and cats were seen in the area.

A few drunks from the local bars staggered down the street after school was dismissed every week. Prostitutes were active in the area usually after school hours. A few managed to be picked up by the "johns" during the day on the corner of Sixth Street and Limestone Street.

Despite the dangerous mix of "people activities", I felt safe at Johnson School. Perhaps, knowing most of the families and several neighbors on Sixth Street contributed to these feelings.

* * *

During the first Christmas holiday of 1985, I chose to work on December 23rd. Principals had the option to work that holiday to catch up on paperwork and phone messages.

My desk faced the only window in my office. The unique view from there was of the side parking lot and the back of Progress Market. I could

47

also see Al's Bar, The Lily Pad Bar, and the Barber Shop. It was busy on the street before lunch that day. While I was looking at this view, "Santa Claus" came out of the Lilly Pad Bar with a girl on each arm. Santa wore a red suit with a red hat and white beard. The girls wore glittery tops, jeans, and high heels.

The three staggered out of the bar and onto the sidewalk. I knew if I told anyone what I had seen it would not be believed. I grabbed the instamatic camera, ran outside, and got their picture just as they crossed Limestone Street to get into a waiting car with a driver. They waved to me as they drove away.

* * *

Two teachers chose to work in their rooms that same day. They were getting their classrooms ready for the new year. The third grade teacher came into the office very upset. "Ms.Michaux, you need to see the illegal act this man is doing on the playground," he said.

I said, "What do you mean by illegal?"

Red faced he replied, "See for yourself. Come to the stairwell and look out the window. Don't let him see you."

We looked out the second story window toward the playground. A man was standing out in the building enclosure with his pants down to his ankles, masturbating. I said to the two teachers, "Why don't you return to your classrooms? I'll call security."

I called security. They arrived minutes later. There was no place for them to park out in the turnaround by the school because there were several cars and a hearse parked there. Security drove their car up onto the sidewalk into the grass. I came out the front door and showed them where the man was standing. At the same time, the front door to the house across the street opened. People came out carrying a casket. There had been a wake in the house. People filed out to get in their cars to follow the hearse to the cemetery.

Security spotted the man and he saw them. He took off running to the back of the school yard with his pants down. They took off after him. The funeral procession was shocked and embarrassed at what they saw. I returned to my office. When I was leaving for the day, I called security and let them know I was setting the alarm. (We called in everyday). The dispatcher said, "Ms .Michaux, they caught your man." (What man, I thought.) Then I remembered. He was talking about the man on the playground.

'Thanks for telling me." I said. He continued. "They caught him on Seventh Street. He had numerous arrests for being a "peeping tom."

* * *

In the late 1980's, classroom phones were installed. A teacher could call another classroom, the office, or make local calls. One afternoon, a teacher called the office in a panic. "Look out the window!" she said. "I'm in my classroom (facing Keller Alley) with my students on the floor. There are two men outside in the alley shooting a gun into the air! Help!"

I called 911 and the police soon appeared. Outside in the alley, two men were arrested for shooting a gun in public near a school. One of the men said in a slurred voice, "We was shootin' them squirrels in the trees." Public intoxication was added to the charges. Thank goodness no one was hurt.

* * *

One of the vacant houses across the street from the school had strange activity during the day. People were coming and going into and out of the house. A large barking dog was tied up in one of the rooms.

I was concerned that some of my students who walked past the house to get to school were in harms way. I called the housing inspector for help. He visited the house that day and posted a sign on the door for the owner to call him. When the owner called the inspector and found out I had made the complaint, one of my van tires was slashed the next morning. (I parked out on the street everyday). I couldn't prove retribution but the dog was removed and no one visited the vacant house anymore.

* * *

Walking out the front door to go to the bank one morning, I saw a man sitting on the base of the school flagpole. He had a grocery cart full of aluminum cans in plastic bags.

"Hello. May I help you?" I asked.

"I don't know. Where am I?" He replied.

"You are sitting on the base of Johnson School's flagpole, on Sixth Street."

"Where is the Horizon Center from here?" I showed him the street. (The Horizon Center was a trailer that stood by the county jail about four blocks toward town, from the school. It was a place where homeless people could go during the day).

"Mind if I sit here and rest a spell?" he asked.

"No," I replied. I wanted to sit beside him and ask him about his life but I didn't. He looked very old and seemed to be in poor health.

The Hope Center was built on Loudon Avenue several years later for homeless men. It gave them a place to sleep and access services that they needed.

* * *

Looking out of my office window one morning, I saw a mattress on top of the dumpster. Out of curiosity, I asked the head custodian about it. He said, " When I came in the side entrance this morning, I found a young couple sleeping on it behind the dumpster. I told them they had to leave and take the mattress with them. Well, they left without it, so I pushed it on top of the dumpster since it was too large to fit in the side opening."

* * *

Through a grant, Johnson Elementary became a <u>Safe School Zone</u> from 7:00a.m.-4:00p.m., every school day. This meant that no drugs, alcohol, gambling, or prostitution could legally occur near the school during these hours. A black and white sign was posted on the front of the building that read <u>Safe School Zone</u> for all to see. (Any school could apply for the <u>Safe School</u> Grant.)

With the cooperation of Fayette County School Security, and the local police force, Johnson had a safe learning environment during the school day. I believed in taking any safety measures that would help keep our students and staff safe at school and in the neighborhood. There were thirteen bars and a few liquor stores within a one-mile radius of Johnson School. School Security (on school property) and the local police (off school property) were called when prostitutes, drunks, or unsavory characters were seen on or near the school building during the day. These uninvited visitors were removed. The <u>Safe School</u> program was very successful at Johnson Elementary.

* * *

When there were evening meetings such as P.T.A., neighborhood associations, and First District Council meeting updates on local issues, lasting sometimes until 9:00p.m., school staff and visitors walked together to their cars. Police were always visible in the area, thank goodness!

The local police canine unit used our building at night, occasionally, for police dog training. A heavily padded officer would hide upstairs or downstairs while the dog searched for him. The dog always found his target according to the police officer who relayed this to me.

* * *

One day, the custodian said, "I can't put up the American Flag. The flagpole chain is gone."

"Please order another one. The flag has to be raised everyday," I replied.

It took three weeks to get another chain and another two weeks for the maintenance crew to install it using a special lift. The new flag pole chain lasted a week before it also disappeared. "What's going on?" I thought. We ordered another chain.

Four days later the custodian came into the office and said, "There is a stray dog on the playground. The kids will be out there for recess in an hour. What do you want me to do about the dog?"

"I'll go out and see if I can catch him. He may belong to one of the students," I said.

"He might bite you," he said.

"I don't want to call the Humane Society if he acts friendly toward me," I replied. We walked onto the playground area where we saw a dog with his chain wrapped around the sliding board ladder. He wagged his tail when he saw us. I unwrapped the chain from the ladder and realized our flag pole chain was around his neck!

It took ten minutes to find the student owner of the dog and fifteen minutes to talk to the parents about the stolen flag pole chain around their dog's neck. No one seemed to know how the chain got there. I gently removed the chain from his neck and the parents carried the dog home. Another flag pole chain was ordered. It stayed on the flag pole the rest of the year.

* * *

One morning at Spaulding's Bakery, across the street from the school, the baker said, "Could you do something about the drug deals going on in here while people are waiting to buy doughnuts? It upsets the customers."

"Perhaps you need to install a video camera in your shop and catch them on tape," I replied. In conversation with a police officer the next evening, after a school meeting, I told him about the baker's concern. I told him that if a video camera was installed on top of the bakery, he could see people engaged in several illegal activities at the four corners of Limestone Street and Sixth Street. I know this to be true from having evening meetings at school. When we walked to our cars we saw drug deals and prostitutes "in action."

During a neighborhood association meeting at the school one evening, a local resident asked me, "Why don't you get the "hookers" off Limestone Street at night since you got them to leave during the day?" I replied," The Safe School Zone project made it possible for the students to be safe during the school day. I didn't do it alone. As a neighborhood association, you all need to get rid of the bars and liquor store. Then the prostitutes will move, too."

* * *

A parent of a Johnson student worked the streets as a daytime prostitute. She asked to meet with me after school one day. Her child sat in the office while we talked in my office with the door closed. "We girls have a problem out on the corner. A new girl is working our spot and she is bad news. She has Aids and is messin' with our "johns." Can you do something about her? (I had seen the girl on the street corner of Sixth Street and Limestone Street. She was very thin, dressed in jeans, a long white shirt, and wore a baseball cap).

I said, "I am a principal, not a police officer. Call the police."

She said, "You made us move during the day. Why can't you get rid of her?"

After she left, I called the police officer who worked our area and shared what the parent had told me. The police were well aware of the illegal activities going on day and night in our school attendance area. Several arrests had been made but that wasn't my concern. Rather, it was the safety of the staff and students at Johnson School.

* * *

One time, out in the shrubs in front of the school, a man was sleeping on newspapers. He had tapped into an old water faucet line that had been closed for years. The man had managed to activate the water flow in the faucet to have a few "mixed drinks" before "bedding down" on some newspapers. At least that was his answer when questioned by the custodian and me.

I said, "You'll have to find other sleeping arrangements which are off school property. " He got up and sauntered off leaving us the newspapers.

* * *

A major problem for the custodian, and a safety concern for me, was picking up used needles on our playground every morning. I feared students would pick up the needles and stick themselves. Several addicts used needles on our playground at night. One addict was "shooting up" and pulling blood back into the syringe.

Seeking a solution to the problem, I told all of the students at Johnson that if they found a needle on our playground, not to touch it. I asked them to tell me where it was so I could dispose of it properly. I said, "I will pay you fifty cents for any needle found on our school property." (Out of my pocket). That was a lot of money for a student in 1985.

In the following weeks I paid several dollars for needles found on the playground. This helped address the problem. When a student showed me a needle on the playground, I put on rubber gloves, picked it up and put it in a special red plastic container.

Earlier in the year, I had requested that a fence be installed in front of the school playground to keep a special needs student from running out into the street. Now I needed a fence to keep the drug addicts off the playground at night. (It was denied by maintenance due to lack of funds).

A local newspaper reporter heard about the needle incident and that I paid students for needles found on the playground. He reported the story in the local Lexington Herald Leader Newspaper. Inside Edition, a television program, read the news report and sent a reporter to Lexington to interview me. We made national news about the "creative" way I solved the needle problem on the playground. A few months later a fence was installed in front of the playground area.

Drug dealers litter Lexington

Middle America has dark side

Associated Press

LEXINGTON — Hypodermic needles litter schoolyards. Drug dealers openly peddle their goods on street corners. Buyers and users favor an area known as "Crack Alley."

This is not a drug zone in a large metropolitan area. It could be almost anywhere across the nation.

But this is Lexington — Central Kentucky — a bucolic area known for its pristine beauty. This is the heart of the Bluegrass country, where expensive thoroughbreds romp through manicured horse farms.

A three-day series in the Lexington Herald-Leader this week documented a dark side to this rich landscape of Middle America.

Photographs and stories gave accounts of police rounding up dealers and users in squalid surroundings while children looked on; dealers being hauled away in squad cars; an ambulance crew wheeling an overdosed teen-ager into a hospital emergency room; a child asleep in a filthy room as a police dog searched for drugs.

Pat Michaux, principal of Johnson Elementary School, won't allow children to touch needles found on school property. As a reward, she paid

The Associated Press

Pat Michaux, principal of Johnson Elementary School, paid students 50 cents for each needle they spotted on school property. Fences now surround the school.

them 50 cents for each needle they spot. Fences now surround the school.

Renay Patton, a mother of five, worries about drug dealers approaching neighborhood children.

"Crazies up there (are) trying to get your kids: 'Do you want to get high?' 'You want to smoke a joint?' 'You want to try some crack?' " she said. "It's bad."

Even the two members of the newspaper's reporting team were approached several times by dealers with questions, "Need anything?" or "Looking for something, man?"

The dealers will intimidate those who try to stop them from selling in the street. Some are part of a network that extends to other large cities.

Near the swings at the Fraternal Order of Police Playground, a 17-year-old boy is found semiconscious on the ground. He had been "huffing" — inhaling — gold spray paint from a plastic bag.

Gold paint covered his lips and oozed from his mouth.

"You wanted to see drugs," paramedic Rick Hisel told a reporter. "This is drugs."

During a raid at a home invested with cockroaches, a child tells a police officer, "We don't got no dope."

The worst areas are Bluegrass-Aspendale and Third and Race streets in the inner city. It's been so overrun by drugs that people can't sit on their porches anymore.

Ms. Patton once saw a drug-related shooting on Race Street.

"They were having a shoot-out up here," she said. "I'm running down the street with a 3-month-old baby in my hands and my kids right behind me. It was ... broad daylight."

The city has responded to the drug problem by adding more police to the street drug task force. In 1989, six drug detectives arrested 619 people. So far this year, 11 officers have made nearly 550 arrests.

"People are telling us in record numbers that 'We're unhappy with the situation that exists in our neighborhoods,' " said Lexington Police Chief Larry Walsh. "The people that cause the most inconvenience, the most discomfort to the community are the street dealers, and we're coming after them."

Walsh believes that as much as 90 percent of the city's crime is committed by drug addicts.

Capt. John Bizzack, who heads the detective bureau, said, "Unless we have educational program behind us — like DARE (Drug Abuse Resistance Education) — we might as well forget it," he said. "Attitudes have got to change."

* * *

A homeless man came into Johnson School one morning. I met him in the hallway. (This was before the doors were locked during the day).

"May I help you?" I asked.

"I came to use it," he replied.

"We are a public school not a public restroom," I said.

He looked me over, eyes moving up and down. "You don't look half bad," he said.

I didn't know where he was going with that comment but I escorted him out the front door of the school. Be darned if he didn't walk around to the library side of the school, and urinate in Keller Alley! All of the classrooms on that side of the school could have seen him.

* * *

One of the strangest events happened at 6:30 a.m., one morning. I looked out the main office windows to see a gray haired woman in a hospital gown running through the front door. Her hair looked like she had put her finger into an electric socket. She was wearing a plastic wristband.

"I'm running for president of the United States!" she yelled.

"You go, girl!" I replied.

"Kill all the Catholics!" she screamed.

"Atta' girl!" I said.

From her appearance, I figured she had escaped from Eastern State Hospital which was on the west end of town. Thus, I agreed with everything she said.

"I need to use your phone!" She yelled.

"There is one you can use on the street corner," I replied. I walked her around the counter, took her arm, and escorted her out the front door. When she left I called the police. They picked her up, thank goodness!

* * *

As I headed out the front door of the school, on my way to the bank, I encountered Marty, grandmother to two of Johnson's students. She was standing outside smoking a cigarette. (It was allowed in the 1980s.)

"Hey, Miss Show. I like your dress," she said.

"Thank you," I replied.

"All I wear are these pants," she said.

"Marty, I'd like to wear pants more often, but it's a mandate from central office that we always look professional."

" A man date? I ain't even got a man." Embarrassed at my blunder, I said goodbye and left.

A few days later in the Family Resource Center, Marty asked, "How was your man date?"

"Fine," I replied.

* * *

Marty walked her grandchildren to school everyday. One day she came into my office while I was doing paperwork. It was the end of the month. Marty asked, "Miss Show, can you loan me one dollar and fifty cents to buy a pack of cigarettes? When my check comes the first of the month, I can pay you back."

"Yes," I replied, and gave her the money. The day she got her check she returned the borrowed money. "Marty, I'll put this money that you have given to me into an envelope and put it in this side drawer. It will be there if you need it again at the end of the month. You'll know where it is in case I'm not here." She hugged me and said, "O.K."

* * *

I received a call from Marty at home one evening. "Miss Show, I can't get Margie out of the tub and into bed. I told her I'd call you but she didn't believe me. Will you talk to her?"

"Yes. Put her on the phone," I said.

"Hello?" a seven-year old voice said.

I sternly said, "Margie, this is Ms. Michaux. If you don't get out of the tub and into bed like Marty told you, you'll spend tomorrow in the SAFE room."

She whined, "I'll go to bed right now."

"Good girl, Margie," I said.

The next day Margie was real friendly to me. There were no more phone calls from grandmother Marty.

* * *

The guidance counselor and I made a home visit after school one day. A parent signature was needed for testing a student for Special Education services.

56

A heavy set woman was digging the contents out of a garbage can. It was sitting near the curb where I parked the van. She was wearing a royal blue coat with a matching lampshade on her head. "Hello Girls, Jesus loves you. Can you give me some money for food?"

"Sure." I said. I handed her five dollars as the counselor rolled her eyes at me.

"God Bless You!" she said. Walking to the parent's house, I said, "I gave her the money because it took a lot of creativity for her to put her outfit together!"

* * *

Before school dismissal one afternoon, the custodian and I approached a drunk man lying face down in the grass, near where parents waited to pick up their children. He was one of our Johnson parents.

"You have to leave because you are drunk on school property," I said.

"No, no, I'm resting 'til my kids come out and I walk them home," he said with a slurred voice.

"You are not walking anyone home in your condition. Go home. I'll call your wife to pick them up when she gets off work."

The custodian and I helped him to his feet and watched him stagger down the street toward his home. I called the students into the office where they did homework until their mother arrived.

I could have called security and had him arrested, but why? What good would it have done? I knew the parent. He was not belligerent to me. He was a very nice person sober. He left the school without incident. The next day the parent came into the office and apologized for his behavior. He thanked me for not having him arrested.

I felt that it was vital that the principal knew the families of the students. It was so much better when everyone worked together for the good of the children, instead of taking legal action in a non-threatening situation. He was sober the rest of the school year.

* * *

Early one day, I walked up the sidewalk, near the school, and noticed trash in the front yard. I walked into the grass, retrieved the trash, and took it inside the building for disposal. A short time later a parent came into the office and said, ""I saw you pick up some garbage in the grass with your dress and high heels on. I now know you care about our kids."

"Thank you," I said. I didn't question what she meant. I simply accepted her compliment. You see, it really was about the children.

* * *

In the 1980's, one of the biggest concerns in the neighborhood that affected the school environment was the presence of gangs. They were visible on nearby street corners during the day, especially after 4:00p.m.,when the whole atmosphere of the inner city changed.

Johnson School had younger siblings of gang members who worried about their older brothers and sisters being shot by rival gangs. They talked about their fears in school. Groups of young people were visible on the street corners when parents walked their children home from school.

In the 1980's, Johnson was a late starting school. (8:55 a.m.) When the parents and children walked home from school, it was 4:00p.m. and the gangs were present on the street corners. I called the local police and asked them to be visible in the area until all of the families walked home. They were always supportive.

The chief of police and I discussed gang activity in the neighborhood. He said that we didn't have gangs in Lexington because they weren't organized like the "Bloods" gang and others who were in California. I disagreed. In my opinion, anytime there was a group of young people who dressed alike, carried guns, vandalized property, beat up homeless people on the streets, and engaged in "drive-by" shootings at certain houses, it was a gang. They called themselves different names for the gang they represented.

People who lived in the inner city were well aware of a dozen gangs roaming the streets at night, and sometimes during the days on the week-ends. The gangs were identified by the way they were dressed. One gang wore a baseball cap sideways on their heads. One gang wore a pant leg rolled up halfway and the other pant leg down. One gang wore bandanas a certain way.

On home visits, bullet holes were visible in the windows of a few rental houses. Some bullet holes had been shot into the house, while others had been shot from inside out.

If a shooting or gang fight happened over the week-end, in the neighborhood, some of the students talked about it in the classrooms on Monday morning. They wrote about it in their journals or wanted to share what went down on the street with their teacher.

It was not a safe time to walk in the neighborhood. Parents were very concerned about the safety of the children walking to and from school.

One of our former students, who was in the ninth grade, came by after school, one day, to proudly announce that he was part of a gang.

"What do you have to do to be part of a gang?" I asked.

He said, "Part of the initiation into a gang was to beat up a homeless guy but not bad enough to put him in the hospital. You have to prove you're a man with a girl. I was shocked but remained calm.

"Does your gang carry guns?" I asked. He didn't answer the question. I knew guns were illegal and he didn't want to comment on them.

"I am now part of a brotherhood. We watch out for each other." He said. The next year, he dropped out of school and was often seen hanging out on the street corners. It was a sad story that was repeated many times by some of our former students.

A few of our parents carried knives or concealed guns while walking to and from Johnson School. One father visibly wore a tobacco "machete" knife that hung halfway down his leg. Security told me it was legal as long as it was visible. The year was 1988, before schools were locked and knives and guns declared illegal to bring into the building. However, during that time of safety concerns, we locked all the doors into the school during the day.

It was common for the staff and me to drive some of the families home after an evening P.T.O. (Parent Teacher Organization) meeting or students' performance at the school. School Security was always visible at evening meetings and the police were alerted to patrol the area at night. I was grateful for the support the local police gave us during the days and evenings.

One of our former students was in the Juvenile Detention Center, on Cisco Road, after a shooting incident on Maple Street, which involved two rival gangs. He told his mother to ask me to visit him. One day after school hours, I did. He looked at me and said, "I don't know why I was arrested and put in here. Two other "brothers" shot him, too."

The victim was a rival gang member who later died at the hospital. Two other gang members were arrested but my former student was charged with murder. His mother was devastated. His younger sister wrote about her brother in her journal at Johnson. The mother and daughter were in counseling for a long time.

* * *

In the 1990's, the gang activity continued in the Johnson School community. One of our former students, Will Carter (real name), was part of a local gang.

Will was a student at Johnson for two years. He was happy at school, well behaved, and eager to learn. After middle school, Will joined a gang in the area. One night, on Toner Street, he was shot by a rival gang member. The "brothers" in his gang ran away. Will fell down on the street and bled to death. Sometime later, a neighbor saw his body and called the police. When they arrived, Will was dead. I went to his wake at a nearby church. Present were women, children, two gang members and I. The only adult male was the minister. What a waste of a young life.

The D.A.R.E. (Drug and Alcohol Resistance Education) Officer talked about Will in the fifth grade DARE classes. He told them that being in a gang was not a brotherhood when a brother was shot, and the rest of the brothers ran away, leaving Will to bleed to death. "Will would be alive today if one of the gang members had called 911 immediately," The police officer said.

* * *

The Johnson School Attendance Clerk made a home visit to the housing projects on East Sixth Street, concerning two truant students who lived there with their mother and her boyfriend. (No phone). As she approached the apartment complex, several police officers and the county coroner were at the scene. The mother and both children were crying on the front porch. The boyfriend, who was black, had been killed by a white police officer. The Attendance Clerk returned to school, visibly shaken and very upset about what she witnessed. The local news reported the incident. The next day, at Johnson, it was discussed at breakfast by several students and staff.

As the school leader, I told the students over the intercom, how safe everyone was at Johnson, and how important it was to concentrate on their studies during the school day.

It was a scary time for everyone in the Johnson community. Out of state license plates were visible on cars up and down the streets near school. Some of the cars stopped families on the sidewalk. Strangers talked to our parents walking to and from school. They wanted the parents to riot against the injustice of the "racial shooting".

With the unrest in the neighborhood, our school doors remained locked at all times. Parents had to come to the school, sign in, and pick up their children. No student was allowed to walk home unescorted. Besides the gangs, groups of adult people were seen on the streets at all hours. Several families were afraid to leave their houses.

The Johnson staff did an outstanding job of keeping the students focused on learning in the classrooms. They assured the students that school was a safe place to be during the school day.

Some of our mothers volunteered everyday at school so they would be safe. They didn't feel safe in their homes with all the out of state cars and strangers in the area. A few of the parents told me that they discussed the rioting idea in their churches and no one wanted any part of it. (Apparently some of the out of town visitors had talked to a few church groups over the alleged "racial shooting").

I asked a local police officer to speak at staff meeting about safety issues involving the staff coming to and going from Johnson School. He taught us safety precautions for getting out of our cars to enter the building, and leaving to go to our cars at the end of the school day. I told the staff to go home after school hours in the daylight. No one was to stay in the school until dark while the unrest in the neighborhood persisted.

The police were more visible in the area and school security was on full alert. Some of the people on the street were arrested and a strong effort was made to regain a safe neighborhood.

Every morning, over the intercom, I welcomed everyone to Johnson School. I reminded them that our school was a safe place to be during the day. I told them that our doors opened at 7:15 a.m. and closed at 6:00 p.m. (There were several new students enrolling each month and their welfare was a concern, too).

Every afternoon, before dismissal, I said over the intercom, "Walkers, walk home with a buddy. Stay on the sidewalks and don't walk in the alleys. If no one is at home, walk back to the school and come to the office."

I pay tribute to my staff who kept the students focused on the curriculum at school. It took a special kind of teacher to teach students in an inner city school. Our teachers were caring people who believed all children could achieve academically. They had high learning expectations in the classrooms regardless of the challenges outside the school environment.

The Knight Ridder News Service in Louisville, Kentucky, wrote an article entitled Inner City Teacher Gets Highest Score in Job Stress. It came from a magazine article in the July/August issue of Men's Health Magazine. The magazine asked job-stress experts to rank jobs based on factors including degree of danger, number of deadlines, amount of competition, and degree of job control. This was defined by whether the job carries a lot more responsibility than authority. Twenty jobs were top listed. The top ten most stressful jobs were:

- Inner-city school teacher
- Police Officer
- Air Traffic Controller
- Medical Intern
- Firefighter
- Waiter
- Assembly Line Worker
- Customer-Service Representative
- Securities Trader
- Newspaper Editor

The magazine suggested that if you were looking for less stressful work, try one of these careers- Forest Ranger, Artisan, Musical Instrument Repairer, Architect, Natural Scientist, Actuary, Piano Tuner, Barber, or Librarian.

Each teacher at Johnson School received this article with a note from me that read, "I appreciate you very much."

Things Happen For A Reason

Before being hired as a principal, I was a physical education teacher and a single parent raising two sons. I also worked part time at a Chevy Chase fashion shop called the "Patchwork Boutique." One cold winter night in December, ten minutes before closing time, a ski-masked man walked into the shop and said, "Do you sell men's clothing?"

I stupidly said, "No. Gee, has it started snowing outside?" I looked out the window and saw that there was no snow. I felt the hairs on the back of my neck stand up.

He pulled out a gun and said, "Give me all the money."

I gladly obliged because there was a gun pointing at my heart. (Also, there was a silent alarm in the cash register).

"Put all the money in one of your shopping bags," he said.

Since there was a gun involved, I followed all of his directions. He was calm so I was also calm. (My youngest son wanted to be like the karate star, "Bruce Lee," so he took karate lessons. While he was in his class, I took a class in self-defense). That night, the self-defense class saved my life, even though nothing prepared me for a gun in my face. After he took the money, he said, "Is there anyone coming to pick you up?"

"No," I replied.

"Is there a back door in the back room?" He asked.

"No," I said, with the gun staring at me.

He took me to the back room where he duct-taped my wrists behind my back, and put tape over my eyes and mouth.

The phone rang in the back. He said, "Are you expecting a call?"

I said, "No."

He then said, "Answer the call but no screaming."

He undid the tape over my mouth and put the phone to my ear. "Hello," I said.

Silence, then click. It was the alarm company. (Anytime the alarm went off, the alarm company called. I had to use my "code name" if it was a false alarm). The masked man heard the click of the phone and hung up the receiver. Before he put tape on my mouth, he said, "Where is your purse?"

"Behind the cash register," I said. The phone rang again. He repeated the same instructions as the first time on how to answer the phone. As he put the phone to my ear, the store manager yelled, "The police are on their way!"

The burglar heard what she said and put tape over my mouth. He walked to the front cash register, saw a police officer out front, and ran back to me. He grabbed me around the neck and walked behind me, pushing my body in front of him. (I learned in self-defense class that when you are grabbed around the neck, from behind, put your chin down to keep from getting choked, so I tucked my chin). He was so scared that I felt the adrenaline pumping in his arm. He had a strangle hold on my chin and neck. He pushed me out the front door and onto High Street in the Chevy Chase area. We stopped traffic. Cars were honking for us to get out of the way.

"Drop it!" the police officer yelled.

The robber shoved his gun hard against my right temple and screamed, "If you come near me, I'll blow her fucking brains out!"

I prayed to God that if I was allowed to live, I would do anything He asked of me.

Then the realization hit me; the gun barrel was plastic! (I had fired guns before and knew what they felt like. My sons had "held me up" with plastic guns playing "cowboys"). As the man dragged me across the street, I picked up my feet and became dead weight. (I learned in self-defense class to become dead weight to avoid being taken to a second location where I could be raped or killed).

He couldn't drag me and also point the gun at the police officer, so he dropped me in the middle of the street and took off running. The police officer told him to stop. When he didn't, the officer shot him, grazing his buttocks. The man went down screaming and hyperventilated. The rescue squad was called. The police officer kept the man on the ground with his gun pointed at his back. An old lady who lived on the corner, ran up to the police officer, told him someone was shooting guns, and that he needed to investigate. She was oblivious to the robber on the ground.

Meanwhile, back in the street, I was on my knees, with horns blowing for me to get out of the way. I yelled a muffled "help" through my taped mouth. A bystander said, "Follow my voice." On my knees, going in the direction of the voice, I made my way to the curb, where hands grabbed me, and pulled me behind a parked car. The bystander took the tape off my eyes, mouth, and wrists. We were crouched behind a car because no one knew who was shooting whom.

Out of nowhere, six police officers arrived on the scene. One of the officers took me back to the shop. "Was the robber black or white?" he asked.

"Neither. He had an accent." (He was Hispanic).

I called my sons to tell them I'd be late coming home. The store owner arrived. We went to police headquarters to identify the shopping bag and retrieve the money.

In court, the accused robber told the jury that he wasn't going to hurt me while adding that he had two years of college. Since I was the only witness, I had to testify. There was extra security in the courtroom since he had threatened to kill me. (I didn't know that until later). The jury charged the man with robbery and kidnapping. The jury gave him ten years for the robbery and fifteen years for the kidnapping. This meant that he could be released from prison in five to seven years with good behavior.

Thank God, that in Kentucky, we have the Persistent Felony Offender law. This law allowed the lawyer to bring up the man's past criminal history. This man had murdered another man when he was sixteen years old. He had also served time in prison in San Antonio, Texas. He had served time for six counts of armed robbery and had recently been released. (It was there that he had received two years of college).

The jury deliberated and added sixty years to each count. This meant that he would serve at least twenty years before being released. He was sent to Peewee Valley Prison in Kentucky. The judge in the case later told me that the convicted man requested being transferred to a San Antonio prison because he liked it much better than the above prison. His request was denied.

The following July, I was asked to be the principal of Johnson Elementary School. I gratefully accepted the position. I truly believed it was the reason my life had been spared.

Flora

Smoking was allowed in public schools in designated areas in the 1980's. A parent, Flora Goins, enrolled her three children, one day at Johnson. She was smoking a cigarette, and "god damning" a few things, too. I asked her to come into my office to put out her cigarette as well as to refrain from using curse words in the school.

She obliged and said, "I quit school in the seventh grade because the teachers were mean. Nobody cared about my education."

I said, "Flora, today is your lucky day. Our teachers will care about your children. They will teach them to read, write, and do math. All you have to do is get them to school on time everyday." She looked at me with challenging eyes. I knew we could win her over to our way of thinking. It just took time.

After the three children were enrolled, they were given school supplies and clothes from the clothing center. Flora told me that she had moved here from another county. She was living in the housing project at the end of Sixth Street. After paying the rent, she had very little money left. Thanks to generous donations of clothing and food to Johnson School, we were able to help her and the children. Since the housing project was within a mile of the school, Flora walked her children to school everyday. (Students who lived beyond a mile from the school were bussed).

While her children ate breakfast, Flora stopped in the office to get a cup of coffee before walking back to her apartment. After a few weeks, she felt comfortable in the school setting.

One day Flora came into my office and told me a very sad story. She had a fourth child, a son, who was removed from the home when he was eighteen months old. She explained that her mother had become ill in another county. Flora had had a friend watch her baby while she and the three children visited her mother for a few days. The arrangement seemed alright until the friend left the baby alone in her apartment one night. Hearing the baby's constant crying, the neighbors called the police. When Flora came home, she had to go to court. She learned that her son had been removed because she put his life in danger. He remained in foster care.

Flora was sobbing while telling me the story. She received a letter stating that her son was going to be adopted at the end of the month. She wanted me to call the Cabinet for Families and Children and talk to the social worker whose name was in the letter. She wanted to see her son one more time before he left her life for good.

I thought, "Dear God, I'm a principal, not a miracle worker. Help me find a way."

Flora persisted, grabbing my arm, and sobbing her heart out until I finally gave in. After introducing myself to the social worker on the phone, I said, "Please bring Ben to Johnson School so his mother and siblings can visit with him one last time."

She replied, "That is against the rules and not allowed."

"Do it any way. I'll be responsible for Flora and the children's behavior."

"Who do you think you are telling me to go against the rules?" she asked.

"Look, this isn't about you or me or the rules. This is about a mother wanting to see her son one more time to say good-bye."

She softened then and said she would work something out although it was highly unusual. A date was set to bring three-year old Ben to school. We met in the conference room. It was a sad meeting. Ben didn't remember his mother but he let her hold him on her lap and hug him. I took several instamatic pictures of Flora and Ben. The siblings came in and hugged and kissed Ben. He liked the attention he was getting from the family.

Some more pictures were taken and farewells were given. There wasn't a dry eye in the room. The social worker was overcome and thanked me for having the meeting. The Polaroid pictures became Flora's memories.

I talked often to Flora during the first semester of school. I was surprised when she came into the office one morning and said, "Ms. Michaux, I need to talk to you in your office now."

We went into my office and closed the door. Flora laid a .38 caliber gun on my desk. I was shocked! Before I could say anything, Flora said, "You've been like a mother to me. There is nothing I have that you would want. I have no money to give you, but is there anyone you want done in?" I was honored, relieved, and still shocked at the same time.

I said, "Flora, please pick up the gun, put it in your pocket. Let's walk out of the school at once. If not, I'll have to have you arrested."

She put the gun in her pocket, and gave me a big hug on her way out of the building. Amazing! I have good friends but none who would kill for me!

Busing

During my leadership at Johnson School, the Fayette County School system used busing to achieve racial integration. As in other United States cities, busing created unintended problems for families because the busing formula was complex.

Johnson School was in an area where students were bused. The black students who lived on certain streets were bused to suburban schools for integration. The white students who lived on the same streets, walked to Johnson, or another school nearby. For example, if you were black and lived on Elm Tree Lane, you were bused to Julia R. Ewan School. If you were white and lived on the same street, you walked the several blocks to Johnson. Students who lived on North Limestone Street, from Third Street to Seventh Street, and lived in even numbered houses, walked to Russell Elementary on Fifth Street. Students who lived in the uneven numbered houses walked to Johnson Elementary on Sixth Street. Children living in the government housing project at the end of Sixth Street were bused to five different schools!

Several of the families gave the school the wrong address for their residences. They wanted their children to walk to Johnson instead of being bused across town. Many of my families had no car, thus, it made sense to the parents to walk their children to the closest school.

As one parent said, "If my kid gets sick at school, how am I supposed to get him home? I don't own a car and can't afford to pay someone to drive me to the school, far away, to pick him up. He's going to go here to Johnson School so I can walk to school and pick him up."

* * *

In August 1992, the Lexington Herald Leader Newspaper wrote an article about twenty years of busing in Lexington- "The Black Child's Burden." It reported that fifteen percent of Fayette County's black elementary school children were being bused out of their neighborhoods to promote racial balance, even though the District was not required to do so. It was a good article that explained different areas in the inner city where black students were bused to suburban schools. In my opinion, it placed a hardship on many of our community families because there was no transportation for the parents to get to and from their children's school.

At Johnson School, with ninety-five percent of the families on free/ reduced lunch, it was imperative that their children walked to the nearest elementary school. It wasn't about racial equality. It was about poverty.

One third of Johnson's parents was 18-40 year old single mothers living on welfare. Families living at or below the poverty line were eligible for Medicaid (medical card) for their children. Another one third was married parents working two jobs with an annual income below fifteen thousand dollars. It was poverty level, but they couldn't apply for children's medical cards because they made too much money. They couldn't afford to buy health insurance either.

Another third was grandparents and foster parents. The grandparents were on fixed incomes while trying to raise their grandchildren. The parents were incarcerated or in alcohol/drug rehabilitation. Health insurance was an issue, although foster parents received medical cards for the children. A few Johnson families had jobs with good salaries, owned their homes, and paid for their children's lunches. They had health insurance for their families.

* * *

One morning, the secretary came into my office and asked, "What is an Aborigine?"

Puzzled at the question, I said, "I believe they are people who live in the bush in Australia."

She replied, "We have one enrolling out here in the office. What race are they?"

"Black, I believe," I said.

She said, "You better come out here and talk to the mother."

I walked out into the main office and introduced myself to the mother and her son.

The mother said, "We just moved to Elm Tree Lane. My husband is a visiting professor at the University of Kentucky."

The secretary said, "Your son is black and needs to enroll at Julia R. Ewan School."

The mother replied, "He is not black, he is an Aborigine."

The secretary looked at me. I said, "Go ahead and enroll the child." (Some situations aren't worth the argument).

I called Fayette County Department of Pupil Personnel to inform them that I had approved a student who was out of district. I explained that the family would only be there for one semester and we had space. In reality, the mother didn't have a car and had to walk everywhere.

* * *

In the early days of my school leadership, when a student was enrolling at Johnson, the father's race determined where the bi-racial children could enroll and attend school.

One day, a white mother brought three bi-racial children to be enrolled at Johnson. It was the middle of September. When she gave her address, the secretary said, "You live in the Russell School area. Your children need to enroll there." (She lived on a street where the black children went to Russell and the white children went to Johnson).

"No. My children are white and they will enroll here," The mother replied.

I asked the mother to be seated. I called the Russell principal and explained the situation. He said, "The mother got into an argument with one of the children's teachers and wanted her child moved to another classroom. I denied the request. The mother got mad at me and withdrew all three children." I thanked him and called Central Office for permission to enroll the students out of district. The family stayed at Johnson for the rest of the year.

* * *

Russell Elementary School was located on Fifth Street. Its families were working poor, middle class, and a few upper class. There were more families with cars; more of their students paid for lunch, and had health insurance through their parent's work place, than our families at Johnson.

The irony of busing black students out of the inner city to suburban schools, located in the south end of Lexington, for integration in the 1980's, was that the south end schools became overcrowded (with new subdivisions being built). Sixteen years later, Fayette County Board of Education had to redistrict students to relieve overcrowding. Their solution was to bus some of the students downtown to schools that were not overcrowded.

An excellent article in 1996, in the Lexington Herald Leader read: Parents tell panel: Don't bus our kids (by Krista Paul, staff writer). Excerpts from the article are…. "Redistricting schools is complicated. But if you ask parents on the south side of Lexington what they think, it's simple. They don't want their children bused. They want them going to school near their homes, in their neighborhoods, and in their communities. And if they're not happy with the redistricting plan, they'll pull their children out of the public school system, many said last night at the first public forum on redistricting."

"I will not send my children to schools downtown. My family will shoulder the financial burden of private school as I'm sure other parents will, too," said one of the parents.

Further down, the article read…. "More than 300 parents and community members, mostly whites from the south side, attended the forum. They came for answers and explanations. They got neither."

In another paragraph the article continued,…. "About 35 people spoke. Most said they bought homes on the south end because of the schools their children would attend. And most insisted that their children would not be bused to other schools.

…".But one of the goals of redistricting is to equalize bussing in the county. Since busing began more than twenty years ago, children have been bussed from downtown outward, and black children had to bear the disproportionate burden of the busing."

The article continued to talk about the short term solution to alleviate overcrowding. It went on to say that the long term goal was to equalize the school system, including who rides a bus, where. …."Still, parents said the redistricting committee should be focusing on neighborhood schools for all children. Neighborhood schools encourage parental participation and give students a chance to take part in more extra curricular activities," they said.

…."Pat Michaux, principal of Johnson Elementary, a downtown school, said that neighborhood schools aren't just important on the south side of Lexington. "Most of my families don't have money to buy homes," Michaux said. "Most of my parents rent. They want to walk their children to a school near where they are renting. They often don't have transportation, so it's important that the school is close to them."

The article continued…"So far, the redistricting committee has decided on four criteria for a successful redistricting plan:

- Giving schools a sense of community
- Making schools diverse
- Limiting busing as much as possible
- Using creative alternatives to redistrict" (end of article.)

The newspaper article was an "eye opener" to many people who had no idea that the school system had been busing the downtown black children out to the suburbs for the past twenty years. For the first time, some of the white parents realized how important a neighborhood school was in the community. Thank you, Krista Paul!

Raven Run

During my first year as instructional leader of Johnson School, four black sixth grade boys created havoc in the classrooms and other areas of school. They gave the middle finger gesture to the teachers, picked up chairs, threatened classmates and intimidated boys in the restroom. I got tired of seeing them in the office, calling their parents, and putting them in SAFE. They were falling further behind in their studies from missing out on their teachers' instructions.

Finally, I called all four boys into the office and said, "It's obvious to me that what we are doing is not working when you misbehave, so this is what we'll do. Here is a contract stating that if you have good behavior for one week or five school days, and finish your class work, I will pick you all up at the school on Saturday, and take you to a special place."

"Where we goin'?" one asked.

"A place where there are no streetlights or sidewalks," I replied.

They were skeptical of me. Here was a white woman principal telling them she would take them on a field trip on Saturday. All they had to do was behave. They agreed. Everyone, including me, signed the contract.

All of the boys returned their permission slips by that Friday. They had been signed by their parents saying that they were allowed to go on a field trip with me to Raven Run Sanctuary. We planned to leave at 9:00 a.m. and return at 3:00 p.m. I told them to wear old clothes and tennis shoes because we'd be hiking. They didn't know what hiking was but didn't ask. All four managed to stay out of the office for the week and finished their class work. Their teachers were amazed.

Saturday morning, I drove the van into the school turnaround at 8:45

a.m. They were sitting on the curb. I didn't know how long they had been there.

"We didn't think you'd show," one boy said.

"Fooled ya'," I replied.

They all got into the van and sat down. We were at Raven Run Sanctuary thirty minutes later. I had on old clothes and tennis shoes and had brought a first aid kit. "Why are you bringing that box with us?" One boy said.

"In case one of you gets hurt," I replied.

We headed for the woods. I stayed on the path starting out. When we had walked awhile, one of the boys said, "Is there anything in here that will hurt us?"

"I don't think so," I said. I noticed all four were staying close to me.

I took them off the path and into a flat rocked creek. It was September and was still fairly warm outdoors. We walked side by side, wading in the cool creek water. "Look at that!" one shouted.

"What is it? They're everywhere!" another yelled.

"They're skimmers," I said. " They skim the top of the water. The salamanders and fish eat them."

"I knew that," the first one said.

When we approached the waterfall I said, "We'll climb down the left side by the waterfall where the rocks are and help each other down. I'll go first and grab each hand coming toward me." I scooted over the rocks and on down to the bottom side of the falls. They were scared, and a few were noticeably shaking, but since I went first, they followed. They didn't know that I had been a physical education teacher and had brought the hiking club here for ten years. When we approached the second waterfall, near the old mill, I told them to watch what I did and follow. I sat down at the top of the moss-covered rocks while water flowed freely over them. I slid down the falls into three feet of water by the old mill rock. I stood up and looked at their wide eyes and gaping mouths.

"Come on, you can do it," I yelled. A sudden transformation happened. Here they came, laughing and playing like eleven year olds. When their bottoms hit the slippery rocks, and they were sliding down the falls, they let out a "war hoop." It was a sight to see. There was a grapevine nearby. I demonstrated how one could swing out over the creek and back upon the bank. We played there until each one had three turns on the grapevine. When we hiked to the halfway point overlooking the widest part of the Kentucky river, one of the students asked, "What is that down there?"

"It's the Kentucky River," I replied.

"Where does it come from?" He said

"From all the surrounding streams and creeks that flow into it," I said. It dawned on me then; we showed these students blue lines on a map at school, and called them rivers, but the students had no idea what we were talking about.

As I was telling the students that the widest part of the river flowed below this overlook, a college student was there taking pictures. The college student turned and said, "Ms. Michaux, are you still bringing students hiking here?"

My goodness, it was Brian Perkins, a former Julius Marks Elementary student who had been in the hiking club. I hugged him and was so glad to see him again. He said, "She was my physical education teacher. She brought the hiking club and me here ten years ago. I am a senior at the University of Kentucky and I still hike these trails, taking pictures."

The four boys were impressed that he was a former student of mine. We continued hiking for two more miles into the woods.

At the end of the trail I said, "Leave only your footprints in the woods. Appreciate the beauty of the forest and leave it like you found it."

We left Raven Run Sanctuary dirty, tired, and in need of food. I drove to the country store in Spears, where we were treated to big fat homemade ham and cheese sandwiches, chips, and a drink. The students hadn't seen a pot bellied stove before or a reward for a missing cow posted on a bulletin board. After we returned to the van I said, "We're going to see the Ferry on the river."

One of the boys said, "Ain't no way I'm gettin' near a fairy."

"It's not that kind of a fairy," I replied. Then they saw the sign "Ferry 500 feet."

I parked the van on the left side parking lot. We all walked together down the road. The boys saw the Kentucky River up close for the first time. Their mouths were wide open as they saw the big paddle on the side of the ferry boat. "Can we go across and back with the cars?" I asked the paddle boat captain." The students have never been on the ferry and I'll be glad to pay the fee." The captain looked at me and said, "You all can stand here on the side of the boat, and watch the paddle get us across the river. We can hold three cars today. There is no fee for all of you."

"Thank you very much," I said, and the students chimed in, "Thank you" with me.

"Look at the ducks over there!" one of the boys cried. There was a family of mallard ducks that stayed on the river by the ferry. The ducks were fed everyday by the people on the boat dock, nearby.

"Here comes a tree down the river!" one boy yelled.

We all watched a big log float by the ferry and on down to the locks. When the ferry crossed the river and stopped on the side of Valley View, the boys watched the cars drive off the ramp, and onto the road. They cheered when the cars drove onto the road and not into the river!

We returned to the original bank. The boys were in awe of the old railroad pillars still standing in the river. The railroad had taken the Bybee Train many years ago, to Whitehall, the home of Cassius Clay. He was a cousin of Henry Clay the Kentucky statesman. Henry Clay's home is called Ashland and is in Lexington.

The hiking club and I had discovered the old railroad tracks that carried the Bybee Train while we were hiking on the side of the hill by the Kentucky River. There were no rails left, just the path and some rotting timber. There was a train tunnel which was still intact, and the remains of an old "moonshine still" on top of the hill near the tracks. We hiked to a big cave that was past the scenic, frothy, twin falls. Kentucky history surrounded us.

We left the ferry. I drove to Daniel Boone Camp Road and parked in the parking lot near the dam and locks. The water was running fast over the falls. We stood near the locks watching the current. The boys were well behaved and excited at the new sights and sounds around them. It was a beautiful fall day. I enjoyed being with the students.

When we returned to school, they wanted to walk home seeing that no parents were there to meet us. "No, I will drive each one of you to your house," I said. I took each one home. Monday morning, at school, they came by the office to say hello. They told me they had had a good time. From then on there was no trouble out of any of the four in the halls and classrooms. I believe that trust was established with the students. They accepted me as a person who cared about them.

The next year, the boys were in junior high. They came by for a visit of remembering the good times." (We had junior highs in the 1980's. Middle school came in the 1990's).

Leadership Challenges

The role of the principal of Johnson School took great dedication and fortitude. There was no course in college that taught me how to work with a high concentration of low socio-economic families. My success in interacting with staff, parents, and students stemmed from my upbringing in government housing in West Virginia. Mother always told me, "You are no better or worse than anyone else. We are all in this life together. You must go to college and make something of yourself."

Three college degrees later, as the new principal of Johnson School, I was astonished at the responsibilities the job entailed. Some of these were:

- As principal, I was the instructional leader. I led and worked side by side with teachers who taught students reading, writing, math, science, and social studies.
- As the instructional leader of the school, I motivated and inspired staff and students to attain high scores on the CTBS (Comprehensive Test of Basic Skills) along with the CATS (Comprehensive Accountability Testing System).
- Another important task was to know how to work within the school budget as well as how to generate additional funds when necessary.
- Additionally, I monitored the implementation of all Title I programs at Johnson. This included weekly testing, progress reports, and budget expenses. Luckily, there was a Title I teacher who collected and reviewed all of the paperwork sent from Johnson to the Fayette County Board of Education office.

- In the Special Education self-contained classes, all students were provided IEPs (Individual Educational Program). Their progress in these areas was monitored and documented according to each student's IEP. Medication was given and monitored for side effects Daily reports were sent home to be signed by parents and returned to school the next day. The Special Education teachers were in charge of the paperwork. Copies of the above had to be made for the students' folders at school, for parents to keep at home. Copies were sent to the Special Education Department at Central Office along with copies of all ARC meetings. From there, copies went to the state and federal government agencies for continued funding. As the principal, I was responsible for it all being done in a timely manner.

- All local District policies and procedures had to be implemented and monitored by sending and receiving paperwork on a daily basis. Before computers were in the schools, all principals had two big blue binders on Fayette County Board Policy and Procedures. Every change in the policies and procedures was sent to the schools. The office secretary, or designated person, had to destroy the old ones and insert the updated new ones in the blue notebooks. After computers, Board policies and procedures were online and updated from central office, allowing staff to concentrate on other job responsibilities. The principal kept the staff informed of policy or procedure changes.

- A principal had to be visible in the halls and classrooms, be approachable to staff, students, parents, and guests, make home visits before and after school, and during school when necessary. Paperwork had to be done after school hours or whenever possible.

- Students' work I believed, needed to be displayed in the classrooms, halls, and office. Art work, murals, and motivational posters needed to be on the walls to be seen and read by staff and students everyday.

- The school had to feel warm and inviting to anyone entering the front doors. Often, I personally greeted parents, students, employees or guests who entered the main office. In the mornings at Johnson School, when the students walked to class, classical music played over the intercom into the halls. It provided a calm atmosphere for the students.

- I felt that it was necessary to have a clean school for all who worked at Johnson. Shiny floors, clean walls, dusted furniture, and a well kept look was a must, even if the school was over fifty years old.

- I was in charge of the building, grounds, and playground. All of these required maintenance and were repaired when necessary.

- As the principal of Johnson, it seemed many times, that I was "putting out fires" during the instructional day. There were incidences where I physically removed disruptive students from the regular classroom, due to fighting or threatening the teacher or fellow students. Teachers had the right to teach. Students had the right to learn. If anyone interrupted the process, he/she was removed from class and sent to S.A.F.E.

- As principal I had to attend many monthly meetings. Some of these were superintendent's meetings, weekly staff meetings, ARC meetings, monthly FRC (Family Resource Center) meetings, weekly S.A.T. (Student Assistant Team) meetings, P.T.O. (Parent Teacher Organization) meetings, and monthly SBDM (Site Based Decision Meetings).

- On Saturdays, at Johnson School, I was in charge of the building from 9:00a.m. –12:00p.m during Saturday School. Transylvania and Georgetown students taught art, music and fun activities to twenty Johnson students in the gymnasium and cafeteria. CSTNC (Community School That Never Closes) offered G.E.D. (General Education Diploma) classes and "Operation Read classes" for adult non-readers during that same time frame and location.

- Johnson's Schoolwide Discipline Plan required that unruly students were sent to the office with a misbehavior form. As the principal, I had to call the parent after talking to the child, or make a home visit, if the attendance clerk was unable to deliver the message. At the beginning of the school year, it was time consuming to call parents. When students who were sent to the office, realized I'd tell their parents immediately to come to the school, less students appeared with behavior forms.

- To be an effective principal, I designated authority to any staff who got the "job done" in all areas of their expertise. I was fortunate to have many outstanding professional people on staff who were team players.
- As Johnson's principal, I had a responsibility to the families in the community whose children attended the school. Johnson was a true community school.

Environment Beautification

One of the responsibilities of the principal was maintaining the school building and grounds. When, for example, the maintenance worker came to inspect the roof, I went up on the roof with him and the custodian. I felt that was part of my job.

Keller Alley was on the left side of Johnson School by the library. Across Keller Alley were two boarded up HUD houses that faced Sixth Street. Big signs saying "Do Not Trespass" were visible on both front doors. Some of the homeless men and addicts loitered on the porches and in the back yards of the houses. The houses were an eyesore. They were dangerous to any students walking in front or behind them on their way to school.

Concerned about the safety of the students and staff, I wrote a letter to the federal public housing authorities and to the mayor's office, asking if the houses could be torn down. I received no reply.

One day after school, one of Johnson's primary students walked behind the houses on his way to meet his mother at the corner market. A man grabbed him and tried to molest him. The child screamed and the mother came running from the corner. The man saw her and ran down the street. The police were called and the mother was able to give a description of the man. He was later found at a halfway house for addicts and arrested.

I was very angry over the incident. I felt I had to take action for our students' safety. I wrote to the Kentucky congressman in Washington, D.C. and told him about the incident. I asked him to help us make the students safe by having the HUD houses torn down. I told him that Johnson School staff and visitors could have a parking lot near the side of the school, on the property where the houses stood.

It worked! I received a letter from the congressman within a month.

He told me that he had pursued the matter with HUD and the houses would be torn down to create a parking lot beside the school. He said that the mayor's office would work with me on the project.

In a few months, the houses were prepared for demolition. The students got to see all of the fixtures removed. They laughed when the bathtub was carried to the truck. Several classes sat in the front school yard and watched the houses being torn down by the wrecking crew. When the bulldozer hit the houses the students cheered!

The dump trucks were a big hit with the primary students. They wrote about the event in class. Many students drew pictures of the trucks and bulldozer. It was a good learning experience for them to observe the demolition. I saw the beginning of a parking lot and students being safe while walking to school.

It is amazing how quickly something can be accomplished when the right people are committed to finding a solution!

LARRY J. HOPKINS
6TH DISTRICT, KENTUCKY

COMMITTEES:
AGRICULTURE
ARMED SERVICES

331 CANNON HOUSE OFFICE BUILDING
WASHINGTON, D.C. 20515
(202) 225-4706

VINE CENTER
ROOM 207
333 WEST VINE STREET
LEXINGTON, KENTUCKY 40507
(406) 233-2848

Congress of the United States
House of Representatives

July 23, 1986

Ms. Pat Michaeux
Principal
Johnson Elementary School
123 East Sixth Street
Lexington, Kentucky 40508

Dear Pat:

I recently became aware of the problems you have experienced with Federal Housing Administration regulations regarding the sale of surplus property homes.

As you know, I recently contacted the District Office of the Federal Housing Authority (FHA) to determine who, ultimately, is responsible for surplus property. To be frank, I discovered a vehicle without a great deal of common sense to drive it. More specifically, I have not been able to identify who actually holds title to this property.

At this point, your patience and persistence regarding this frustrating matter is to be commended. Furthermore, I want to assure you that I will continue to pursue this matter with FHA officials in Washington. If you have any further questions, please do not hesitate to contact me.

Yours very truly,

LARRY J. HOPKINS
Member of Congress

LJH/jbc

HOUSE OF REPRESENTATIVES
WASHINGTON, D.C. 20515

LARRY J. HOPKINS
KENTUCKY

December 17, 1987

Dear Pat:

I am honored that you would think of me at a
time when Johnson Elementary School needed help
to preserve its learning environment and protect
the personal safety of its student body and staff.

In as much as the circumstances you described
fall under the jurisdiction of local authorities,
I was pleased to be able to contact Mayor Baesler
on your behalf.

His prompt call to you and his offer to take
the time to meet and discuss the problem you are
experiencing is exactly the response we have come
to expect and I am confident that with your personal commitment and the Mayor's hands-on leadership,
a solution can be found.

I want to assure you of my continuing interest in the success of your mission at Johnson
Elementary and hope you will contact me whenever I
can be of assistance.

With warmest personal regards, I am

Sincerely,

LARRY J. HOPKINS

Ms. Pat Michaux, Principal
Johnson Elementary School
123 East Sixth Street
Lexington, Kentucky 40508

* * *

First impressions of a school are very important. The front yard at Johnson Elementary looked desolate and uninviting. No landscaping was visible in the yard in 1985. It was devoid of shrubs and flowers. It was an eyesore compared to other schools where I had taught as a physical education teacher.

One Saturday, I was at Colonial Garden Center talking to the owner, Fred "Boots" Bramlett, about the forlorn front yard at Johnson School. He said, "I attended the original Johnson School on Fourth and Limestone Streets, and went to the new Johnson on Sixth Street when it was built in 1939. What do you need?"

Surprised, I said, "You went to Johnson? I'm the new principal there."

He said, "Congratulations!" I thanked him and said, "We need shrubs, flowers, and trees to begin our beautification of the front yard. I have about fifty dollars in donations to spend."

"Do you realize how many shrubs you can buy with fifty dollars? About two," he said.

"Oh," I replied.

"I'd like to donate some landscaping to my alma mater. I'll bring you some bushes," he said.

Early Monday morning "Boots" brought a truckload of bushes and a purple plum tree to be planted in the front yard. He taught three sixth graders how to use gloves, shovels, dig holes, water, and rake. They had big grins on their faces because they had never planted anything before. Mr. Bramlett showed them how to dig a big hole and put the bushes into it. They loved to water the bushes and cover each one with dirt. The students followed his directions until the plum tree and every bush were planted.

Mr.Bramlett said to the students, "These are your bushes and plum tree. If you take care of them, they will be here long after you have graduated from high school." The students agreed to take care of them and thanked him for teaching them how to dig holes and plant for the first time in their lives. Thank you, Mr. "Boots" Bramlett!

* * *

I spoke to a few other garden centers the following year about a county-wide A.P.P.L.E. (Alliance of Programs and Partnerships for Lexington Education) Program. Hillenmeyer Nursery chose to be our business partner for one year. They taught the students about landscaping and how to grow many kinds of flowers, shrubs, and trees. The students learned about horticulture. They visited the garden center and learned how seedlings become plants. A few of the employees talked in the classrooms about horticulture as a job. This helped the students understand that when they grew up, horticulture could be a business that made money. Several fifth and sixth graders were chosen to be gardeners in the spring and fall at Johnson School. They planted donated forsythia bushes on the side of the school by the playground where they bloomed in a haze of sunshine in the spring. Many more students planted pansies, petunias and geraniums in May. Mums were planted in the fall of the year, out in the front yard. Our school yard was beautifully landscaped. There was a lot of excitement about the benefits of the partnership since many of our students lived in rented houses and didn't plant anything outside.

People in the community enjoyed the landscaping. They often stopped in the office to tell us how pretty the front yard looked. There was no vandalism whether school was in session or not, because everyone took ownership in the landscape.

One year, in the fall, a pine tree was donated and planted in the front school yard. The third grade students made seed balls and popcorn garland to place on the tree branches in December for the birds. When they read about Johnny Appleseed, Hillenmeyer Nursery donated two apple trees. The teachers and students planted the trees on the side of the school yard. They read where one apple seed could grow into a big apple tree. The students celebrated by writing poems and stories about apples.

During Saturday School, some students volunteered to water the plants, flowers, and shrubs. They really enjoyed "accidently" squirting each other with the hose!

In December, that same year, I drove to Hillenmeyer Nursery and purchased a van full of colorful red, white, and striped poinsettas. Several of the potted beauties were displayed in the office and cafeteria. The atmosphere was festive and inviting. Staff members bought the rest of the plants for friends and family.

* * *

In the front foyer of Johnson School, stood a giant tropical tree. It was donated by a local paint store. The owner was going to throw it away. I told him that the school children would enjoy taking care of it. He brought it to the school and it lived in the foyer for sixteen years.

In the three stairwells of the school, big windows provided light which helped donated tropical plants grow. Different students were selected to help the custodian water all of the inside plants. The children and staff enjoyed watching the plants grow and thrive.

As the school administrator, I connected with many generous business people who donated a variety of gifts to the school. Some of these included plants, trees, used computer paper, old notebooks, and anything else they were discarding that the students could use.

A local artist painted a beautiful mural masterpiece in the middle stairway. It depicted African American heritage.

One of our art teachers and several students in the art club painted murals of famous cartoon characters in the front stairwell. In the back stairwell, the Art Club painted murals of jungle animals. All the stairwells were very colorful. They made folks smile as they came up and down the hall steps. Visitors remarked on how beautiful the art scenery was in the school. Johnson School had many talented art students thanks to the art teacher who had a passion for teaching it. The students enjoyed art projects and were proud of their work.

* * *

One time when I visited a school in another county, I was impressed with the self-serve food line in the cafeteria. There, students were allowed to choose a selection of food and put it on the tray themselves. In most Fayette County schools a server handed the students a tray full of food. The Johnson cafeteria manager liked the self serve idea because it freed her workers to present a variety of colorful healthy entrees which appealed to the students.

A self-serve line was implemented the following year. Students chose one item from each of the basic food groups. A cafeteria worker monitored the students to make sure they were following the self serve rules in the line. A few staff members didn't like the idea of the students picking up their own tray and putting food on it. They worried about spreading germs even though the students washed their hands before getting in line. I understood their concerns. However, I felt that two important benefits were that the students learned the different food groups and were able to make their own choices of foods to eat.

* * *

The cafeteria walls were nondescript until Southland Christian Church's youth group decided to do a service project there. With the assistance of some Johnson students, they painted a mural on the main cafeteria wall. After school, and on the week-ends, the youth group and our students painted a beautiful underwater scene in the cafeteria. It was complete with a sunken ship, a whale, a shark, and many, many fish, all brightly colored in a sea of blue. We were so proud of the mural! We appreciated all of the hard work and long hours that the Southland Church Youth group and our students gave to create this special work of art.

* * *

I believed that the school environment needed to be pleasing to the staff who worked there and the students who attended there. Visitors were impressed at the warm, inviting atmosphere. The positive impact that the murals, landscaping, and tropical plants had on everyone spoke volumes. Parents believed that the warm school environment showed that the staff cared about their children. The employees also enjoyed working in the colorful environment. Visitors expressed positive comments about the school's appearance.

However, a serious problem still existed outside of the front of the school. The front yard was beautifully landscaped but the six tall windows in front were covered with beige painted concrete. With all the other improvements, they looked drab and out of place. It was obvious that they had been windows, but due to vandalism during the first renovation, they were sealed. I visualized pictures of children painted in each of the window panels. I presented my idea to the staff and P.T.A.(Parent Teacher Association) in September, 1995. They liked the idea but only if there were donated funds to pay for the project. In 1996 my dream became a reality.

It so happened that the substitute art teacher commented on how nice the inside murals were. I mentioned the ugly concreted windows in front of the school and how I had a vision to put two big colorful children from different cultures, in each panel. The slogan would be "Children First at Johnson Community School." "Would you be interested in painting a project of this proportion?" Her eyes grew large. She wanted time to consider the request. Later in the day she agreed to do the murals for a fee. Next, I sought donations for funding and art supplies from several businesses, clubs, and art enthusiasts.

Ms. Holcomb (real name) exceeded my expectations! Her murals depicted two elementary children from different cultures, in each of the six panels. She worked from a scaffold, painting the figures after school and on the week-ends. People in the neighborhood stopped to watch her paint and made very positive comments. One woman driving down Sixth Street, saw the murals, stopped her car, and came into the office. She said that the paintings and front yard were beautiful and handed me a fifty dollar check to be used for anything the school needed!

The local Herald Leader Newspaper interviewed Ms. Holcomb in an article entitled <u>Woman's School Mural Focuses on Children</u>. The article read: "More than twenty years ago, the facade at Johnson Elementary was dominated by six huge windows. Vandals broke the windows which led to their being blocked with concrete panels. Now, where the windows reflected the surrounding neighborhood, the panels show a different world."

Mrs. Price, a neighbor, who sat on her front porch, across the street from the school, watched the whole process. She was delighted to observe the work of art and told me so everyday!

* * *

Another section of concreted windows was on the side building of Johnson School. A few years later, with donated funds, two local artists agreed to paint children running through a rainbow of colors on each panel. These provided a continuation of colorful art on large window panels of the school. The ten forsythia bushes underneath the murals came alive with "yellow sunshine" each spring. Thus, there was artistic beauty inside and outside the school.

The improvements in the appearance of the school helped make it just as attractive as schools in other places in Fayette County. In newly built schools, landscaping was part of the building project. The newer schools had P.T.A. landscaping committees. The principals there didn't have to worry about seeking funding for it.

In addition to the outside grounds, newer schools had updated classrooms which were complete with nice desks, tables, and chairs. They had whiteboards in addition to the blackboards. Those principals didn't have to take time for fund raisers to buy the items for the staff and students because they were already there. As the leader of Johnson School, I believed our staff and students deserved the same benefits that the newer schools had.

* * *

Another important area of the school was the playground. Johnson's playground consisted of one small slide, a geometric dome, swings with frequent broken chains, and a horizontal ladder. The P.T.A. saved fifteen hundred dollars to buy a new set of equipment which totaled sixty-five hundred dollars to build the first part of the total playground.

One spring Sunday, in the late 1990's at Southland Christian Church, the minister talked about VBS (Vacation Bible School)) which was starting in June. I spoke to the minister afterwards about having Johnson School playground be the mission outreach program for the students in VBS. I suggested that the children could help raise funds for our playground. I also agreed to come and talk to the VBS children to share information about Johnson School students. I wanted the church families to visit the school during the summer. While there, I would give them a tour of the building and playground. This was very important to me because I believed that most of the church families had never visited an inner city school. My prayers were answered. The VBS decided to make Johnson School's playground their mission. It really was all about the children!

Thanks to Southland Christian Church, our students would have new playground equipment on which they could play seven days a week. At VBS, the Southland Youth Minister organized a variety of donations to our school. One day, they brought bars of soap and shampoo to the students. The next day, they brought school supplies. The third day it was tissues and band -aids. Another day they provided toothbrushes and toothpaste. On the last day, they donated boxes of detergent. Each day, I took all the donations to Johnson School's Family Resource Center where the volunteer mothers organized them for the following school year. Everyday at VBS, I invited the parents to visit the school.

One afternoon, a VBS mother and her two children followed me to Johnson. When they entered the school building and walked down the hall to the office, the mother remarked about how clean the school was. She was surprised to see the latest technology in all the classrooms. She was shocked to hear her children tell me that they would like to attend Johnson School!

As I was escorting them out the front door to the playground, the custodian stopped me to ask a question inside the door. Just outside, the mother turned around and started beating on the front door to come in. I was puzzled but opened the door. "What's wrong?" I asked.

She said, "There are four black men walking down the street toward the school!" Fearfully, she pulled the children inside the door. I walked out the front door where there were four teenage boys walking past the school. "Hi, Ms. Michaux," they said, "Hi, Guys," I replied. The mother looked at me red faced and said, "I'm sorry. I panicked when I saw them. People don't walk down the street where I live."

I saw fear on her face. She was in unfamiliar territory and was afraid. I told her there was nothing to fear as I walked her and her children to the playground. The children played on the rusted equipment. The mother said, "You certainly need new playground equipment." I walked them to their car and waited until the mother drove off before I went back into the building. She never visited the school again.

All week long at VBS, I wore several shirts with the same design on the front. It read "Children First." The last day of VBS, I asked if there was any question about Johnson School. One third grader asked, "Everyday you have worn the same shirt. Are you poor, too?"

The Vacation Bible School raised sixty-four hundred dollars to buy new playground equipment. The equipment was installed with a big ceremony on the playground. Thank you Southland Christian Church Vacation Bible School.

* * *

In 1998, Johnson School received a fitness course grant which utilized one side of the playground. It was from Project Fit America (A non profit corporation dedicated to health and fitness). Funding for the fitness course was made possible by Central Baptist Hospital. Over twenty-five thousand dollars was donated. Project Fit America installed paths and equipment for both Arlington and Johnson Schools. Part of the equipment included parallel bars and balance beams along the paths. Many of the parents and students used the course on the week-ends. We were a true community school.

Educating the Educator

Four children, who were in foster care with their grandmother, attended Johnson School in the mid 1980's. Their mother was serving time in prison for fatally shooting their father during an argument. The two younger children witnessed the murder. Three years later they enrolled at our school. Tara, the sister, was shy and withdrawn. The brother, Carl, fought everyone. The older brother and sister were better adjusted but had tempers that flared up in class.

Grandmother never came for conferences with the teachers about the children. Many notes went home from the attendance clerk asking her to come to the school to meet with the children's teachers but she refused. I decided to pay her a visit about Carl's fighting and the anger issues of the two older children. She welcomed me into her home. In the living room, I sat down on a plastic covered chair while she sat across the room on a plastic covered couch.

"I'm havin' a terrible time with them grandkids. I take a belt to em' if they get out of hand. If Carl gives me any lip I take a belt to his behind. He minds me then. I don't leave no marks."

"Ms. Hicks, I said, "please do not whip him with a belt. It is physical abuse and against the law."

"You don't understand what I've been through with them. I don't have enough food to feed everyone 'cause my 'lectric bill is due."

"We have a food bank at the school. Come to the school today and you can have what you need," I said.

As Ms. Hicks continued talking about her monetary concerns, she rolled up a newspaper, stood up, and walked toward me, talking the whole time. Raising the newspaper over her head, she hit the wall behind me. WHACK! A big squashed roach was visible on the newspaper when I opened my eyes. Ms. Hicks continued talking through the scenario. She returned to the couch without batting an eye. When she finished the conversation, I thanked her for her hospitality and said, "Ms. Hicks we'll work with you to improve Carl's behavior; meanwhile you come to the school and get the food that you need."

I left the house and got into the van. I thanked God that I had kept my wits about me and hadn't screamed when she came toward me with a rolled up newspaper.

The next month, Carl chipped one of his front teeth in a street fight during one week-end. Monday morning, at school, he was very upset because his tooth was jagged and hurt his lip when he talked. "Carl, the tooth can be fixed. We can sign a contract that states that if you have good behavior, and finish your work, I'll take you to the dentist, and get your tooth fixed free of charge. Will you agree?" I asked.

"Do you really know someone who'll fix my tooth free?" He asked. "Yes," I replied. "Dr. "Oakie" Newsome (real name), my dentist, donated his services to help my families with emergency dental concerns." "I'll do it," he said. I wrote a contract, read it to Carl, and we both signed it. His behavior improved and he completed his work at school. The dentist fixed his tooth and Carl avoided fighting on the street.

Carl went to middle school the following year. Three years later he visited me one day after school. "Miss Show, you gotta' help me. Ma got out of jail six months ago and she's back on the [white] stuff. She's sold everything in the house. I had to sleep on a bench behind the store so she wouldn't sell my tennis shoes. I got to call her parole man and get her back in jail before she gets killed." I dialed the police department and gave him the phone. Carl knew the parole officer's name and talked with him. Afterwards, he thanked me, gave me a hug, and left. Carl didn't return to visit again.

Carl's sister Tara, who was much younger, changed from shy and withdrawn to angry and aggressive in the third grade. One day, Tara and Vera were sent to the office for fighting in the lunchroom. They were still fuming when they sat down in the main office. I looked at pouty lips, squinting eyes, and crossed arms ready for battle. I escorted them into my office. "Before we start talking, you two need to calm down and take a deep breath. Relax your arms and faces." I demanded. "Vera, you tell me your side of the story; when you're finished, Tara, you tell me your side."

Vera whined, "She called me the "B" word so I hit 'er."

Tara chimed in, "She called me the "H" word so I hit her back."

"What does "H" stand for?" I asked.

Tara said, "Hoe." (I thought, does that mean whore).

I said, "Tara," "Hoe" starts with silent "W" not "H." It's the "WH" sound that starts the word "whore." (Oh, no! Here I am teaching these girls to spell whore.)

More sternly, I said, "Fighting is against school rules as is name calling. You two will eat lunch in SAFE for the rest of the week. I'll call your parents and tell them what happened. They can talk to you about this when you get home from school today."

Vera said, "We don't have a phone."

I replied, "I'll make a home visit. I know where you live."

She cringed and said, "Tara and I are friends. We won't fight no more."

Tara agreed. They were not sent to the office the rest of the semester.

The next year when Vera was in the fourth grade, I was in her classroom when all the girls watched a film on menstruation. Several of our girls had started their periods in the third grade which was a little late to see the film. Since I had been a health teacher before I was principal, the teacher asked me to be present, especially during question time.

After the film, the students wrote questions (no signatures) for the teacher and me to answer. Several questions were about sexual intercourse during pregnancy, having a period, and "doing it." Vera stated, "Your brother doesn't count. If you have sex with your brother you won't get pregnant. If it's anybody else, you'll get pregnant."

I said, "Yes, your brother does count. And yes, you can get pregnant having sex with him."

Vera was surprised. "No kidding?"

I was stunned, "It's the truth."

The teacher answered the next question. I was unaware of so many challenges facing our young girls. I later found out that some of the brothers and sisters shared sleeping areas due to lack of beds and bedrooms in some of the rental places.

In the fifth grade, Tara and Vera were sent to the office for "extortion." They were charging girls ten cents to use the bathroom. One of the terrified girls who didn't have any money told the teacher. Tara and Vera were suspended for three days.

When they came to the office on the fourth day, I looked at both girls and said, "You all have to quit threatening the girls in our school. You both are smart and could be leaders of your class if your attitudes improved. Middle school won't tolerate your behavior next year, so you need to change it now. What can you both do to change your behavior?"

"We could leave the other girls alone," Vera said.

Tara said, "We could stop fighting everyone."

"That's a beginning. I'll make a contract with both of you about your behavior goals. If you achieve them in four weeks I'll do something special for you," I said.

"Will you take us out to eat?" Vera said.

"Sure. Where do you want to go?" I asked.

Tara said, "Not to a "burger" place. Can you take us to a place where big people eat?"

"Yes," I said.

We all signed a contract. One month later, with improved behavior, we ate at a south end restaurant. When we were seated the waiter put our wrapped silverware on the table. Vera said, "Why are there diapers on the table?"

"Those are not diapers. They are cloth napkins. The silverware is wrapped up in our napkins. We place the napkins on our laps." The girls unwrapped the silverware and placed the napkins on their laps. Tara said, "Why do we have two forks?"

"In case you order a salad," I said.

"I don't want a salad," she said.

'Then don't use the extra fork," I replied.

The waiter brought menus. I explained all of the different choices of meals to order. Both of the girls ordered hamburger, fries, and a soda. Our orders came, and as we were eating, Vera said, "Why does that man stare at us all the time?"

I explained, "He is our waiter. He'll refill your drinks and remove your plates when you have finished your meal."

Tara said, "I'm taking mine home to show Granny what I got to eat."

"Fine. We'll ask the waiter for a doggy bag to take home, " I said. Vera wanted one also.

We stopped at an ice cream shop and ate ice cream on the drive home. They thanked me for the dinner before they went into their houses. The girls continued to improve in class. They were seldom seen in the office except to say hello. The next year they went to middle school. In the spring they came to Johnson to put their school pictures on the picture board in the main office.

My Staff/Dedication

Throughout the sixteen years as Johnson's principal, I distributed many positive quotes, cartoons, (motivational publications, tapes, and CDs were written down on paper) and placed them in the staff's mailboxes. Any positive reinforcement was shared freely with the staff.

Several staff members thanked me for the "pieces of sunshine." Some told me that they helped get them through rough times in their lives. Whatever the issue, through a divorce, the death of a loved one, or family crises, those pieces of inspiration helped.

I cared about my staff. We had disagreements over the years, but we were united in the goal of helping the students succeed academically. We worked as a team for the students' best interest.

Students who needed extra help in reading and math stayed after school for a one on one with their teachers. Dedicated teachers worked with the students until the subject matter was learned. It was not uncommon to see teachers teaching students who were struggling academically for an hour after school. Since most of the students were walkers, the parents allowed them to stay. Either the teacher or I took the student home afterwards. Many students enjoyed being there because teachers had snacks to eat!

Several teachers had incentives in their rooms for academic excellence and good behavior which were purchased with their own money. The staff spent over seven hundred dollars each year on treats and incentives for their students. Some of these funds paid for pizza parties rewarding one hundred books read, and ice cream or popcorn for good behavior by the whole class. The incentives were for academic success and good behavior.

When local pizza and hamburger businesses gave students free meals to reward academic excellence, perfect attendance, or one hundred books read, the teacher, with the parent's permission, drove those students to get the free meal!

I don't think the general public has any idea how much teachers do to help students improve their academic skills. Johnson Elementary was blessed with many outstanding teachers and staff over the sixteen years I was principal.

* * *

A music grant for ten keyboards in the music room, taught the students how to read music and play the piano, thanks to a very talented and creative music teacher. The five-year program was a huge success at Johnson because our students enjoyed music- singing, playing, and dancing. When the students were in the fourth grade, several took violin at school because they knew how to read music sheets. Others joined the band in the fifth grade, learning how to play different musical instruments.

* * *

In the 1990's a new concept appeared in the workplace. It was called "casual" day or "dress down" day for staff on Fridays. Our staff wore casual clothes to work on Fridays- blue jeans, sweatshirts, and tennis shoes.

Johnson School had a dress code requiring all staff to look professional because school staff were the role models for the students, parents, and guests. The staff adopted the "casual" day on Fridays and informed all of the students and parents of the change. It worked really well until a teacher dressed "casual" on another day, also.

One day when visitors were in the school observing students in the computer lab, one of the visitors said it was nice that I allowed the custodian access to computer time with the students. Of course, it was the teacher in the class that he was talking about. She had worn old jeans with a hole in the knees and a sweatshirt. The sad thing was that the teacher knew we were having visitors that day. I talked with her later, during her planning time. She said, "I have been depressed and didn't get much sleep last night. I overslept and grabbed the first thing I saw to wear to school."

"May I remind you," I said, "you are a professional, and you are to dress as one Monday through Thursday. If you are depressed, call the Employees Assistance Program (EAP) and get help today. It's free to you. You are a valuable teacher to Johnson School." She called EAP after our meeting and went to see them after school. Later in the week, she was much improved.

The Employees Assistance Program was free to all employees and helped school employees in multiple areas of life's concerns. Thank you Fayette County Board of Education.

* * *

Staff meetings were mandatory, every Tuesday, after school, as written in the Fayette County Board of Education policies and procedures book. Each of our meetings had an agenda so that we could stay on task and finish in one hour.

On Friday's, all principals received a principal's packet from the Board of Education elementary director's office. Copies were made containing information that the staff needed to know for Tuesday meetings. (Before e-mail).

During several staff meetings, I did "fun" things to lighten the mood of staying after school hours. One time, I started the meeting by throwing a piece of wrapped chocolate to a teacher. I said it was a "kiss" for having a nice smile. She then picked up another piece of wrapped chocolate, threw it at a teacher, and told him it was a" kiss" for being positive all the time. He threw another piece of wrapped chocolate to a teacher, and gave her a "kiss" for bringing him a cup of coffee that morning. Soon everyone was throwing pieces of wrapped chocolate and giving "kisses" to each other! There was a lot of laughter before the meeting started.

One Tuesday, after a very intense staff meeting concerning testing preparation and testing schedules, I thanked the teachers for their dedication and hard work. I said, "To reward all of you, there is a surprise taped under your chairs." Chairs were picked up and turned upside down. Some teachers bent over with their bottoms high in the air to look underneath their chairs. The surprise was one dollar bills taped underneath their chairs. Three chairs had a five dollar bill taped to them, and one chair had a ten dollar bill taped to it. All bills were randomly placed and the "hoops" and "hollers" were loud! Teachers were most appreciative of anything out of the ordinary.

At one staff meeting, the staff put their social security number on a blank piece of paper and placed it in a can on the table. At the end of staff meeting, we drew the numbers out of the can. From the drawing, the teachers got executive desks, filing cabinets, bookshelves, and stations which were three sided panels, hooked together, around a desk placed for a student who wanted to work alone in class without distractions. There were also padded chairs on wheels. (A local bank downtown, remodeled

100

their offices, and asked me if I could use their used furniture at Johnson. I said, yes, and they sent a truck full to the school). The teachers were very excited with all of the furniture. Several teachers were ecstatic about having a nice desk and chair in their classrooms.

* * *

With parents' permission, one of our first grade teachers brought a bunny rabbit to school for her classroom. It was a floppy- eared rabbit complete with a cage, food, and water bottle. The students learned about its habitat and how to take care of it. The rabbit was paper trained, and ran around the room, after school, while the teacher worked in the classroom.

A few months later, with parents permission, another first grade teacher brought a donated spotted rabbit with a cage, food, and water for her class to school. One day after school, the floppy eared rabbit hopped down the hall and "visited" the spotted rabbit in the nearby classroom. The two teachers thought it was cute to watch the rabbits "play" together. A few weeks later the spotted rabbit was pulling out her fur and making a nest under the heating unit in the classroom. Three baby rabbits were born soon afterwards. Both classes voted on bunny names. Three happy students took the babies home when they were old enough. (Parent permission). We later found out the floppy- eared rabbit was a male, and the spotted rabbit was a female!

* * *

Three creative second grade teachers decided to have an all night, read-a-thon slumber party at Johnson School. All of their students had read one hundred books. The students voted to celebrate with a school slumber party.

On a Friday evening after school, the second graders read books in the cafeteria and ate dinner while the teachers read books to them. Afterwards, the students took turns reading to each other. The blankets, pillows, and donated sleeping bags were spread out on mats on the gymnasium floor. One of the teachers' husbands was the local fire chief, and also a chaperone. My big dog, "Cinders," a Bouvier Des Flandres, also was present.

In the evening, the students changed into pajamas and sat on the mats reading books. Everyone had the opportunity to read. When students needed to use the restroom, a teacher and "Cinders" walked with them.

Several students took turns reading to the dog; little hands petted her as they read the stories all evening.

One of the evening highlights involved students talking over the intercom during break time when snacks and drinks were provided. Any student who wanted to make an announcement for all to hear went into the office and talked into the microphone. "Will (name) please come to the office? You have been bad today! "(giggle, giggle) After students had called all of their peers, they called the teachers and me to the office. What fun!

In the morning, the students had cereal, milk, and a big fat, juicy doughnut from nearby Spauldings Bakery. Parents came to the school later in the morning and picked up their children. It was a good experience for all of us.

* * *

Through a grant with the Living Arts and Science Center, on Fourth Street, in May 1994, Heather Lyons (real name), an artist in residence and independent filmmaker, visited Johnson School's fifth graders three times a week. She taught them how to use a video camera and how to write a documentary about their neighborhood.

Students interviewed business owners, community senior citizens, and a local historian who talked about famous African Americans buried in the African Cemetery #2 on Seventh Street. The fifth grade teachers supported the students' filming in the neighborhood with discussions in class. The students videotaped children playing in the play area at Duncan Park, different architectural designs of houses and buildings, a quilt blowing dry on a clothesline, in the bright sunshine, and interviews with some of the students. They were positive about the neighborhood because their family and friends lived there. The documentary was edited by Ms. Lyons. The local television station, Channel 18, aired it in May 1994. It was well received by many local residents in the Johnson community.

* * *

Another year, Johnson School received a grant from the Living Arts and Science Center. This time our fifth grade students got to be a part of an archeological dig at Kinkead Street and Illinois Street. This was the place where the first black subdivision was built in Lexington. The houses were razed to make way for the extension of Rose Street. The students found hand blown bottles, old utensils, and other artifacts from years gone by. They were taught how to carefully dig and move the dirt. This opportunity gave the students a chance to be a part of a very important time in history. I was glad our students had participated.

* * *

Two of our certified teachers had swimming pools on their home property. Once a year, each teacher invited all their grade level to their houses to swim and eat dinner.

All of the students got into the shallow end of the pool whether they could swim or not. Those students who could swim, jumped off the diving boards. Towels and extra swimsuits were available although a few students went swimming in shorts and tops from home. The staff and I went swimming, too. Some of the students were surprised that we knew how to swim!

* * *

An exciting educational trip that the sixth graders experienced in May 1988 was organized by an energetic sixth grade teacher.

At the beginning of the school year the sixth grade students studied Kentucky caves. The only thing they associated with caves was the big drainage pipes underneath the streets. Some had crawled through them when the water was low. When the teacher discussed Mammoth Cave and how people from all over the world visited the famous place, the students could not imagine why anyone would choose to walk around a hole in the ground.

The teacher came into my office and said, "Our sixth graders need to visit Mammoth Cave in May. I received information from the lodge there, and they can accommodate the students and teachers for a nominal fee. We can have bake sales, wash cars, and anything else to raise the money for all the students to go. The students can bring in small amounts of money each month toward their payment for the trip. By May we'll have enough funds to go."

I supported the field trip, and after approval by the local board of education, letters went home to the parents with the information. Some of the sixth graders who moved out of our district during the year continued to attend Johnson because of the May trip. Some of the teachers' friends donated money for all the students to go on the trip. Some of the students were new to Johnson's sixth grade and didn't enroll until a few months before the May trip. Every sixth grader went on the trip. All behavior problems disappeared when there was a change in the environment. Thus, the students were well behaved.

We rode the bus four hours, from Lexington to Mammoth Cave, in western Kentucky, on a private tour bus. The students were excited about the plush seats and portable bathroom. We sang songs most of the way which were led by the music teacher.

When we arrived at the lodge, the students went to their pre-assigned rooms. The excitement of seeing two double beds, and a shower brought giggles, laughter, and happy faces. Sadly, some of our students had no bed at home, or had only a bathtub with no shower. (Jumping on the beds were against the rules). We preached good manners. I told them that if we showed good behavior, we'd be invited to return the next year.

In the dining room, the students watched the adults who were properly using their silverware and napkins to eat. Some had never eaten in a restaurant and didn't know what to do.

On the visit in Mammoth Cave, many students were fearful, and clung to the closest chaperone. The cave guide, who was very knowledgeable about the cave's history, talked about the underground wonders. At one point, the lights were turned off to show all of us what the early explorers and Indians faced in the cave. It was pitch black! Hands and arms grabbed me in a tight grip!

The lights were turned on again, and the students overcame their fear as they studied the beautiful formations. We heard water in the cave. The guide told us that in the distance there was a river that ran underground. Water dripped from parts of the ceiling. We walked through a narrow space called "fat man's misery" to reach other rooms in the cave.

Before bedtime, the students played in the showers until there was only cold water. Some tried to jump on the beds. Giggling was heard in the halls. Chaperones patrolled the halls until there was silence in the rooms.

The next morning we visited a living cave nearby. We observed albino insects living in the cave. After lunch we returned to school with tired, happy students.

Through the years, middle school students visited Johnson and reminisced about the fun they had had on the Mammoth Cave trip. I was most appreciative of all the staff who took time away from their families to make the trip possible for our students.

* * *

One of our superintendents invited principals to visit his home every Christmas holiday. He and his wife decorated trees with different themes in each room of their house. His wife was a former teacher. She invited some of Johnson students to her home for "Teddy Bear Tea" after the holiday vacation. A student was selected from each classroom for January Student of the Month. (students of the month were those who had good behavior and progressed academically). The guidance counselor and I drove the winning students to her house. They were so excited to visit a beautiful home with all the decorated trees in each room.

One tree was loaded with teddy bears in all shapes and sizes. In an upstairs bedroom we saw an antique dollhouse with furniture. The dolls were from the wife's childhood along with a tree decorated with characters from a famous children's book.

The students were impressed that there were three bathrooms, a tree in every room, and all kinds of antique dolls and toys. We were seated in the kitchen. We had teddy bear cookies and teddy bear tea (milk) while the former teacher read a teddy bear story. The students felt special and thanked our hostess on the way out the door.

In the van on the drive back to Johnson School, the students chatted about how rich the people must be to have trees in every room of their home. One student asked, "How come that grown up lady still plays with baby dolls?" I realized that many of our students moved often and didn't have heirlooms.

* * *

For a spring retreat, the fifth grade teachers took their students on a two-day environmental education trip to the 4-H Camp in Carlisle, Kentucky. Most of our students had not spent the night away from home, much less, in the woods. It was a good learning experience for all the teachers and students. They gathered firewood, cooked over an open fire, made "some mores," (graham crackers with roasted marshmallows and a chocolate bar in between), and stayed out in the woods throughout the day and evening. We played games, sang songs, listened to the noises of the night, and heard stories from the camp director.

A midnight hike up a big hill was a challenge. We laid down on the hilltop to gaze at the stars in the sky. "There are a thousand stars in the sky here in the woods. There aren't many stars in the city sky," one student said.

The camp director said, "Yes, there are. There are the same thousand stars in the city sky as there are in the woods; you just can't see them because of all the streetlights and car lights."

We returned to the cabins. The boys' cabins were on one side of the camp, the girls on the other side. The showers were a treat since many of the students had only bathtubs at home. The rows of showers in one place were a novelty. The girls' showers had curtains, and the boys didn't. The boys' shower experience ended up in horseplay. The men chaperones reminded them to wash!

Before we went to camp, I asked the students if anyone wanted to sleep in donated sleeping bags by the campfire, with me. I told them we'd sleep under the stars, near the lake, and that I would keep the fire going all night. Ten boys volunteered. (The girls wanted to be in the cabins). I told the ten boys that we'd sleep in our clothes in the sleeping bags outside.

When bedtime came, the ten students and I placed the sleeping bags in a circle around the campfire. The boys nestled into their sleeping bags and said how warm they were. As the talk quieted down, the night sounds started. Bullfrogs croaked and a few ducks were stirring on the lake. Crickets were singing with leaves rustling nearby. I had to reassure a few boys that we were safe. As the fire embers died down, I added more wood.

By early morning, the dew was everywhere. I awoke to a low fire and ten sleeping bags huddled around mine! Sometime during the night fear overcame the sleepers.

In talking to one of the teachers the next morning, she said, "In our cabin, the girls put all the bunk beds together so they'd be an arm's reach from the teacher in case any "creature" came through the door. I told them nothing was going to get them but they wanted to be close "just in case."

We ate breakfast in the rustic lodge. The students were divided into small groups afterward. One group learned about the habitat of Kentucky birds with a slide presentation. Then, they walked outside to observe the nests first hand.

Another group walked into the woods and learned how to preserve the environment. One group studied native trees and water creatures. The last group went canoeing on the lake. The groups rotated until everyone had been to all four.

We returned to school in the late afternoon with tired, happy students. I appreciated all of the teachers who took time away from their families so that our students could have this experience. I believed that our students needed to be exposed to experiences outside of the inner city which had positive effects on their lives.

* * *

For an academic incentive, the guidance counselor and I took four of our top achieving fifth grade girls to a local mall, one Saturday, to see Marjorie Judith Vincent (real name), who was the 1991 Miss America. Each student talked with her and received a signed picture. The girls were impressed. She inspired them to do their best in school. They maintained straight A's for the rest of the year.

* * *

One of the highlights around the Christmas holiday was "Shop with a Cop." Fifty students, kindergarten through fifth grades, were chosen by their teachers, counselor, and principal to spend one hundred fifty dollars each, at a designated super store, the Saturday before holiday break. Several staff members and I accompanied the students on the busses for this event each year. A medical group also sponsored a trip to a local athletic center. Here, the students played on an obstacle course, danced, and ate pizza.

Then we went to a superstore where the police officers and helpers took each student shopping. One student's mother gave him a list of things to buy for home. (Detergent, soft drinks, etc). I took the list and told the student that this event was for HIM.

All of the students bought gifts for their families as well as themselves. Volunteers wrapped the gifts and placed them in big plastic bags with the child's name on them.

The parents were waiting at the school when we returned. They were most appreciative that their children had gotten to participate in the event. I had great admiration and respect for the medical group and the police department who sponsored it. They went far beyond the call of duty to make the students' holiday a happy one. (People helping people).

* * *

When I was a physical education teacher in other schools in the county, all of the students experienced lots of educational trips throughout the school year. Teachers collected field trip money from the students before the trip. The few students who couldn't afford to pay went anyway, courtesy of P.T.A. (Parent/Teacher Association) funds.

I included this because as Johnson's Principal, with over 90% of the students on free/reduced lunch, there was little or no money collected from the students for field trips. A minimal amount was given for trips through the Equity Fund for underprivileged students, but it wasn't enough funding to help our students throughout the school year. I strongly believed that our students needed educational and cultural enrichment beyond the classroom, so the solution was to find more trip funding.

When orphanages closed in Lexington the organization that funded them continued to financially assist people/groups in need. I heard about them and the good deeds they did in the community. I wrote them a letter about the needs of Johnson students. They asked me to speak to their group. I did. I explained the need for educational and cultural enrichment through field trips, incentives for academic achievement, and perfect attendance. They gave the students at Johnson the needed funding. For the next two years our students benefited from their generosity!

With some of the funds, the third graders studied transportation and rode on a train in Bardstown, Kentucky. Many parents chaperoned because they had never been on a train either. The fifth graders visited Shakertown, in Harrodsburg, and rode a big paddle boat on the Kentucky River.

The fourth graders studied Kentucky History and visited Fort Boonesborough. Through this, The pioneer days were re-lived for them. They also visited the State Capitol in Frankfort. On their way back to Johnson School they visited the State Game Farm. A few students brought money to play the "video games" at the Game Farm. They were surprised to learn there were only wild animals there!

The kindergarteners visited the Louisville Zoo each spring, thanks to one teacher saving aluminum cans through the school year, and selling them at nearby Baker Iron and Metal Company to pay for the trip. Some of the donated funds paid for two buses.

First graders visited the University of Kentucky Agricultural Farm and saw huge dairy cows, sheep, and pigs. Several petted the baby animals. Second graders had community field trips. When they couldn't walk to an educational event, they rode a school bus.

Johnson School teachers extended educational learning experiences through field trips from the classroom to the community and other counties. For many of our students, the field trip was the first time they had ever been outside the inner city. They were in awe of the sights!

When a class took a field trip, the digital camera went along. I recorded pictures to download on the computer later at school. Each student wrote what they learned from the pictures and the writing piece was placed in the student's writing portfolio.

In the main office, there was a bulletin board that displayed pictures of students and staff on field trips, reading in class, and in the computer lab. Visiting guests and community residents' pictures were also displayed. Everyone who came into the office enjoyed looking at the pictures on the community picture board.

* * *

Through a reading grant from KDE (Kentucky Department of Education), a reading teacher worked with our teachers on different reading strategies. The specialist also taught reading to some of our students.

It was late October; the reading specialist and I were discussing Thanksgiving in my office. I remarked, "Our students do not understand that the turkey they eat on Thanksgiving is the same turkey they color with feathers, a head, and big feet. A lot of them believe a turkey is pink skinned with no head or feet. I'd like to find a real turkey to put in a cage in the hallway, by the front office, to show the students what a turkey looks like and how it acts."

She smiled and said, " I have a turkey on my farm. When I was a classroom teacher I had a cage and took the turkey to school to visit. I'll bring you a turkey and a cage the week before the Thanksgiving holiday so the students can observe it." I was elated.

The second week of November a real caged turkey arrived and moved into the front hallway for all to see." I refuse to clean out the turkey cage," the custodian grumbled.

"That's fine. I'll do it," I replied.

Everyday, in my suit and pantyhose, I got down on my hands and knees, pulled the soiled papers out of the cage, and replenished them with new ones. I was pecked by the turkey a few times but it was worth the experience. Students helped change the water and put in corn feed. All students going to the gymnasium and library passed the turkey cage.

"He sure shits a lot," one student said.

"That's because he only eats corn," another student replied.

"Yeah, when I eat a lot of corn I get the shits, too."

I appeared in the hallway and said, "Quit cursing out here in the hall."

I heard, "O.K."

Every time the front hall doors opened the turkey gobbled loudly. After a week of observing the "watchdog" turkey, the office secretary was ready to take a hatchet to him!

The students drew turkey pictures, learned how a real turkey looks and acts, and wrote about the kinds of sounds he made in the hall. Students' turkey pictures were hung in the hallways. They read about the habitat of the turkey and wrote poems about him. There was a Thanksgiving program with student participation followed by a big dinner in the cafeteria. The staff ate dinner, family style, with all the students. The reading specialist took the turkey home. Over the four-day holiday some of us ate ham instead of turkey!

* * *

Johnson School Staff created and implemented a Schoolwide Discipline Plan, kindergarten through fifth grade. With the guidance of a central office coordinator, Johnson School's plan was effective and successful!

* * *

One of our teachers helped a Johnson parent who wanted to become an elementary school teacher. She helped the parent get a loan, enrolled her in the University of Kentucky, and bought the books she needed for classes. Every morning, the teacher picked the parent up and drove them both to school. The parent drove the teacher's car to classes. After class, she returned to Johnson to volunteer in the classrooms. When the parent graduated in the top of her class we all celebrated at school. She later became a primary teacher at Johnson.

The teacher went far beyond the call of duty in supporting the Johnson parent. I was grateful that the parent was on the Johnson staff. Empowering the people is the best solution to break the cycle of poverty.

* * *

CHARLES BERTRAM/HERALD-LEADER

Michelle Sleet prepared for the new school year in the room where she taught primary grades last year. Her new classroom, where she will teach fourth graders, wasn't ready.

Johnson Elementary inspired parent to get degree and become a teacher

During my leadership, many applicants were interviewed for certified teaching positions. The interviewing committee included several staff members. For example, if a teaching position was open in the fourth grade, a fourth grade teacher, the counselor, a parent, and I made up the committee.

We did not hire an applicant who said, "I just love to work with poor children," or better still, one who said, "My husband really doesn't want me to work down here."

The real shocker came when one applicant had the gall to say, "I just want you to know that I'm interviewing at … school, too, and even if I get this position, I can't accept it until I hear from the other school."

The teacher who had high expectations for academic excellence, wanted to teach children, and was not concerned about the above issues was the one we hired.

The same questions were asked of each applicant by the committee members. When the applicant left we discussed the positive and negative answers that were given. Our goal was to hire the one who would best teach, care about, and understand our students.

When the decision to hire a candidate was made, I called the references that the applicant had provided on the resume. Most of the time the references were honest and positive about the applicant. There were a few instances, however, when I felt that the principal wasn't truthful in the evaluation of the applicant. I suspected that the principal was giving me a glowing report of a teacher he or she wanted to see leave.

Interviews were sometimes not what they seemed to be. Some of the applicants talked very professionally, were positive, and appeared to know about the position they were seeking. After they were hired, however, they turned out to be the opposite teacher type for the position.

That's why references were very important. I refused to be a reference for any employee for whom I could not give a positive evaluation. Many principals were given positive feedback from me about teachers who transferred from Johnson School to a school in another county or state. One principal called a month later, from another county, to thank me for being honest about a teacher transfer. He was most impressed with her leadership and training not to mention that she was an outstanding teacher.

It was vital that we hired teachers at Johnson School who wanted to be there. Our students deserved to be taught by the best teachers and staff who made educating students their highest priority.

Before direct deposit of teachers' paychecks, they were delivered by courier on payday to the school, and placed in the individual mailboxes by the secretary or me.

On several occasions, I delivered the paycheck to each teacher's classroom, handed the paycheck to him or her, and thanked the teacher for teaching at Johnson School.

The students sometimes said, "Do you have one for me, too?"

"Yes, if you stay in school and get a college degree in teaching, and teach here, I'll give you a paycheck, too," I replied.

Sometimes students said, "Why do you thank the teachers for working here?"

I replied, "I am grateful to have teachers who want to be here teaching you. They will help you will realize how successful you can be. How would you learn if there were no teachers to teach you? Be thankful that you have good teachers who care about your education."

The teachers appreciated the positive comments from the principal about their teaching and commitment to educating their students.

In 1986, the State of Kentucky's General Assembly mandated "duty free" lunch for all certified teachers and classified assistants. This meant that the staff ate lunch in the teachers' lounge or workroom, or their classroom, for twenty-five minutes, while their students ate lunch in the lunchroom. "Duty free lunch" freed teachers from having to supervise students during the students' lunchtime.

Funding was available to hire two lunchroom monitors for two hours, everyday, to supervise the students eating lunch. I hired two of our grandparents as lunchroom monitors during the first year. They knew several of the children's parents and were wonderful role models for them. If a student misbehaved, one of the monitors said, "I'll tell your mother how you're acting and you'll be in double trouble."

The lunchroom rules were posted in the cafeteria. Any class exhibiting good behavior during lunch earned a star by their teacher's name on a big behavior chart hanging on the wall. After two weeks of stars by the teacher's name, the class was rewarded with ice cream, their favorite treat!

Classified employees were very important at Johnson. They provided necessary support to students and teachers which helped strengthen learning. Johnson School had over thirty classified part time and full time employees who worked different hours each day of the week.

An incident happened one week that warranted the installation of a time clock at Johnson School. One of the part-time custodians didn't show up for work at his scheduled time. When he arrived two hours later, he said, "I parked up the street and have been in the building all the time you were looking for me."

I replied, "No, you were not in the building nor was your car parked up the street. You didn't sign in, either."

"I forgot," he said. "You didn't see me but I was here."

This issue occurred one more time. I called the director of maintenance and asked if he could come to Johnson to greet the custodian when he arrived for work the following day. He was waiting for the custodian when he showed up two hours late the next day. He was told the same story I was told the day before.

The custodian was reprimanded by the maintenance director for arriving late to work and not signing in at the office. If he had been honest about being late, I would have worked out something with him. Instead, he chose to lie. He quit his job at the end of the week.

The majority of the classified employees signed in and out of the building in the front office. The problem was that the secretary and other office workers had a lot of work to do and couldn't monitor who was present and who was absent. To simplify monitoring of classified staff hours, a time clock was purchased with fund-raised money. This allowed all classified employees to clock in and out on a time card, everyday. There were no more problems with attendance issues.

* * *

As principal, it was a challenge to monitor the attendance of thirty-five certified staff. The majority was always on time, arriving thirty minutes before school started. Several teachers arrived an hour before the school day began. I walked the halls many mornings and observed who was on time and who was not.

The head custodian arrived at 6:00 a.m. He did a security check of the school before any teacher was allowed into the building.

When the students were sent to their classrooms from breakfast in the cafeteria, teachers stood in the hall and greeted them. When students were lined up by a closed classroom door, I knew that their teacher was having a parent conference or was running late. If there was a conference, it gave me the opportunity to open the door, and stop the conference so that the teacher could welcome the students to class. If the conference needed to continue, the teacher scheduled it for another time. The teacher's first priority was the students in the classroom.

There were a few teachers who were often late. After discussing the attendance concern with them individually, they got to work on time. Teachers had children of their own who went to other schools in the district. They drove them to their schools before coming to work.

Walking the halls in the morning gave me an opportunity to talk with teachers who didn't come to the office during the work day. After school, when time permitted, I visited teachers working in their classrooms. There, I heard concerns which I would not have heard had I not visited them at that time. I made a real effort to be approachable to staff. It worked for me.

Teachers in each grade level had common planning time to discuss curriculum, testing, and educational field trips. I was available to meet with the different grade level staff when possible.

In January 1989, Eastern Kentucky University invited me to speak at the Phi Delta Kappa (honorary group) meeting for students who wanted to be teachers. Since I received two degrees from Eastern Kentucky University, I wanted to "give back" to my alma mater.

The topic was about the urban setting for teachers and my experiences as an inner city principal. I was honest about the challenges of teaching low socio-economic students. I was also positive about the students' success through elementary years when caring teachers have high expectations for them. Sharing funny stories about the students, teachers, and myself was an important part of my speech. I wanted the students to know that as teachers they needed to "be themselves." They needed to know that academic expectations were expected along with caring about the students. Hopefully, hearing about my experiences inspired the students to be excellent teachers after graduation.

* * *

Over the years our students were given awards for academic excellence. The A and B honor students received a monetary reward with an award certificate after every nine-week grading period.

Students received one dollar each for perfect attendance. They also got a chance to have their name drawn to win a bicycle. There was one for primary students and one for intermediate students every nine weeks. Parents were invited to the assemblies to watch the awards given to the students. These were monetary incentives for our students to excel and many improved every nine weeks. School attendance improved with the bicycles because the majority of our students had never owned a bike. All of the reward funds were donations from organizations that supported our incentive program. However, a few parents and staff members didn't agree with the incentive program. I heard, "In my day students learned without getting anything. It was expected of them." I believed that it worked for our students.

* * *

Johnson School had a "Gifted" program for five third through fifth grade students who excelled academically. The "Gifted" teacher came every Friday for extra instruction.

* * *

Every nine weeks teachers scheduled conferences with their students' parents, only to have a low turnout. A few teachers had two or three parents show up out of a class of twenty-five students. Others had none. This happened despite letters being sent home with scheduled times to meet with the teacher. Parents were also asked to call the school for an appointment.

Thinking of a solution to the problem, I met with a service organization that wanted to do an outreach program for people of poverty. My plan was simple. I asked if they would sponsor a dinner every nine weeks for our families. The only stipulation I had was that the dinner had to be held at the end of the month when some of the welfare checks were spent and food stamps were scarce. I knew the families would come to the conferences to get a good, hot meal. Several parents came for conferences every nine weeks; but we needed all of the parents to visit their child's teacher every nine weeks.

A letter went home to the parents. It stated that if the parents would come for a parent/teacher conference at the end of the month, the teacher would give them free dinner tickets. This meant that the whole family could eat dinner free of charge. The menu was spaghetti, salad, rolls and cake. Coffee, tea, and milk were served in the cafeteria.

It was a huge success! Not only did parents come for the conferences, but grandmothers, boyfriends, cousins, and anyone else living in the home came, too. They sat in the hall outside the classroom until the parent conference was finished. Then, all ate together in the cafeteria.

Parents and friends appreciated the meals and expressed their positive feelings to the service sponsors. In one year, our parent attendance to parent/teacher conferences tripled!

Students were happy to see their parents talking to their teachers about their academic progress. Our parents cared a great deal about their children's education. They felt more comfortable at school every nine weeks because of the generosity of one service organization.

There were groups of people in organizations who helped our school because they knew it helped the children and their parents. I was fortunate to find them for our families.

* * *

In April 1989 in the Sunday section of the Herald Leader newspaper, an article appeared about Johnson Elementary School and my role as principal.

In addition to the issues I faced during the instructional day, the article talked about the dedication of the teachers and staff to improve their students' education while also dealing with many social issues in the community. The statewide newspaper article was well received with many complimentary letters sent to me by educators. However, I also heard from some of the local black leaders who were upset about my negative comments concerning the area surrounding the school. I acknowledged their complaints but firmly believed that "you can't fix what you don't acknowledge." I felt there was a lot of "fixing" to do in the community.

I believed that the principal of Johnson was not only the instructional leader of the school but also a well informed leader who knew the families and their environment in the community. There were grandparents raising grandchildren who instilled good values and self esteem in the children. There were also welfare parents, working parents, and foster parents struggling to do the best they could. Even though many families were poor, there was structure, involvement in education, and love in their lives.

I thanked God for the dedicated staff at Johnson School who worked with the students and their families. It took years of training, hard work, and commitment to witness our students' academic excellence on the state tests and continued improvement every year.

State Superintendent of Public Instruction, John H. Brock, from the Kentucky Department of Education, wrote a letter to me (on the following page) after reading the article about our Johnson staff in the Herald Leader. Thank you, Dr. Brock.

COMMONWEALTH OF KENTUCKY
DEPARTMENT OF EDUCATION
FRANKFORT, KY. 40601

JOHN H. BROCK
SUPERINTENDENT OF PUBLIC INSTRUCTION

April 25, 1989

Ms. Pat Michaux
Principal
Johnson Elementary School
123 East Sixth Street
Lexington, Kentucky

Dear Ms. Michaux:

I have just finished reading the article in the Lexington Herald about you and your work at Johnson Elementary. I was deeply moved by this article which so vividly reflected you and your staff's compassion and dedication to the students and parents of Johnson Elementary. So often we "administrators" get caught up in our world of meetings, fiscal years, and legalities that we loose sight of what is happening in the real world and particularly in the world that you work in each day. It is so refreshing to see how you approach what some would see as insurmountable odds in educating these children.

I hear every day, sometimes over and over again, what is wrong with education in Kentucky. You and your staff are shining examples of what is right in education in Kentucky. You may not always be "successful," the statistics may not always reflect positive achievements, but Johnson Elementary is a standard for all of Kentucky's schools to meet. The standard of a warm, caring, and safe environment where children are free, for a few hours at least, to learn. Thanks, Pat. You've made my day.

Sincerely,

John H. Brock
Superintendent of Public Instruction

An Exciting Day

Early one morning, a Johnson cafeteria worker who lived in the area came into the office and calmly said, "There's a dead man layin' in the alley out by the school."

Startled, I asked, "Where?"

"Out there before you turn into the parking lot," she said.

I told the secretary to call 911 since the body was off of school property. I called the head custodian to go with me to find the dead body. The man was laying by the alley on a filthy mattress that had been discarded for trash. I yelled at him to get up. No response. He didn't move at all.

The police and rescue squad arrived. The police officer yelled at the man to get up. Nothing moved. The rescue person got down in his face to check his breathing and take his pulse. The man's eyes opened. When he saw all of us around him he shot up off the mattress, and wailed. We looked very intimidating to him I'm sure. "I was just sleepin'," he said. Do you have a cigarette?" His hands were shaking badly.

After I realized that he was alive, the custodian and I returned to the building across the alley. Thank goodness he was alive and no students who walked to school had seen him there.

A police officer came in later and told us that the man on the mattress had consumed too much cheap wine the night before. He said that the man had no idea how he landed on the mattress in the alley.

* * *

Later in the morning, a young copier repair man ran into the school building with a splotchy face. He was sweating profusely and was in a state of disbelief. I asked, "What is the matter with you?"

He shakily said, "I parked in the parking lot on the side of the school. When I started to get out of the car, a woman jumped in on the passenger side and asked me, how do you want it?" I didn't know what she was talking about.

"Want what?" I asked. She told me that for five dollars I could get a blow job and for ten dollars she'd sit in my lap and do me. I was so scared! I screamed at her to get out of my car and I ran in here. Is she still out there in my car?"

One of the office employees looked out the side window and said, "No, there is no one in the cars out in the parking lot."

I said, "I'll walk you to your car if you want to lock it. From now on, lock all your doors before driving into the neighborhood to visit Johnson."

He looked at me and said, "Don't worry. I'm never coming back here. They can send someone else!"

* * *

One of our fourth graders in the Intermediate Resource Room ran into my office at 10:30 a.m., on the same day, and cried, "Miss Show, come and help the substitute in our class. She's crying."

I followed Larry to the classroom and sure enough she was crying at the teacher's desk. The rest of the students were sitting quietly in their seats. "What's wrong?" I asked.

She sobbed, "No one told me I had a different lesson for each kid. I can't teach all these different kids."

I said, "No, you probably can't. Boys and girls, please get your lessons out of your folders, and return to your regular classroom. The substitute is leaving."

She said, "Thank God!" She collected her purse and coat and left the building never to return to Johnson School.

* * *

At lunchtime, nine year old Evan had ten dollars for extra food. "Where did you get your money, Evan?" I asked, as we sat down with our trays in the cafeteria.

Evan said, "Miss Show, I found two big plastic bags full of dead grass under a house (basement) and a man saw me draggin' 'em down the street. He paid me ten dollars for 'em. He sure was stupid."

I thought, uh, huh. Evan found someone's marijuana stash, stole it, then sold it. I was glad Evan wasn't hurt in the process.

* * *

After lunch the same day, the head custodian was outside mowing the grass. The assistant custodian was at lunch. A call from a first grade teacher was desperate. "Jason has vomited all over the rug and on one kid's shoes. Help! We all have the "dry heaves" and he isn't through upchucking!"

In my high heels and suit, I grabbed the kitty litter bag, broom, and dust pan, and hurried to the classroom. The smell hit me first. All of the children were sitting in the far end of the room away from the vomit. Some had their heads down and one was crying. Jason was heaving liquid out of his mouth. The teacher was trying to clean him up with paper towels.

"Take the rest of the students outside into the fresh air. Jason and I will be O.K. here," I said.

The teacher and students quickly exited the room. I took Jason to the sink in the room and washed his face and hands. He was exhausted and embarrassed because of the vomit that was everywhere. I put kitty litter on the spots in the rug. Soon, a clean smell permeated the room.

"Jason, are you feeling well enough to go to the Family Resource Center to get clean clothes?" I asked.

"Yes," he said.

After he put on clean clothes I told him his mother was on her way to take him home.

"Would you like to sip on a carbonated soda while you wait for your mother? It may help settle your stomach," I said. He was drinking the soda when his mother showed up and took him home.

The teacher took her students to the library and read books until the custodian finished cleaning the classroom.

What an exciting day and it was not even dismissal yet!

Montey

One of our foster families lived a block from the school. The five children who lived there were well behaved with one exception, ten-year old Montey, who had anger issues.

In class he would explode, yelling obscenities, and refusing to do his work. Weekly counseling at school wasn't addressing his sudden outbursts. One week, he was in SAFE three times.

His foster mother was frustrated. She had a doctor examine him. Montey was put on medication and eventually was calm in class, but the anger outbursts still occurred.

"Montey, what we are doing for your negative behavior is not working," I said on his third office visit in one week. "Is there anyplace you would like to go or anything you would work for to end your angry outbursts?"

Montey's eyes lit up and he said, "I'd like to go to the race track and live."

I asked, "Why?"

"'Cause Mom and me lived there before they put me in foster care," he said

I was astonished. I had no idea that this child had been exposed to life on a race track, much less, that he had lived there.

"OK, Montey. Here are the terms of your contract for good behavior. For the next two weeks you will behave appropriately, have no office visits, and complete all class work assignments on time. At the end of the two weeks, if you fulfill your contract, I will pick you up on Saturday morning and we will visit the race track for two hours. To make this contract binding to us, we both have to sign it. Agreed?"

"Yes!" He replied.

I called his foster mother to explain the contract. She readily agreed to it.

"You really would do this?" Montey asked.

"Yes," I said, and for the next two weeks I did not see his face anywhere near the office.

His teacher said, "I hope you fulfill the contract because Montey is hell bent on doing his part. He has finished all of his class work and is a nice student. Sometimes I see his face puff up, and he has fisted hands with the tight knuckles, but he keeps it together."

He fulfilled his part of the contract and with the written permission signed, I picked him up on Saturday. We headed for Keeneland Race Track to enjoy a beautiful fall day in October.

Upon arrival, a different Montey emerged from the van. He was grinning from ear to ear. He grabbed my hand and started running to the main gate. It was 7:30 a.m. The crowd had not arrived yet. I bought hot chocolate and doughnuts for us. We sat on a bench near the track.

The announcer called out the name of the horse who was warming up on the track. We watched a beautiful horse run by. The lather was visible where the reins had rubbed its neck. There was foam around the horse's mouth. He seemed to enjoy the freedom of the wide open space.

Montey was giggly and happy faced. He seemed so glad to be there. We drank the hot chocolate and ate all of our doughnuts.

Montey looked at me and said, "Miss Show, see how the rider leans forward on the horse?" I nodded yes. "They do that to get the best running time."

"Can we go to the stables?" he asked.

"Sure," I said.

Montey took my hand as we walked past the stables and into the open area. A horse was walking around in a circle. Its halter was attached to a rope on a pole which was hooked to a center pole. Montey said, "The horse is being cooled down."

There was another horse standing with a groom. "See the bandage on the horse's leg? He has some soreness there. He has to heal up before he runs again," he shared.

I wished that his teachers could have heard him. He was very knowledgeable about the horses and very comfortable in his surroundings.

"Where did you learn so much about horses?" I asked.

He was silent for awhile and then stated, "Mom and me lived out here in a trailer. Sometimes I slept in the stalls. I learned a lot from the horse doctors and trainers. I know a bunch of horse stuff and how to play poker, shoot craps, and bet on the races. I want to be a jockey when I grow up."

Two hours went by quickly before I took him home. He thanked me for taking him. I thanked him for teaching me so much. If a school course was offered on horse care and training, Montey would have been at the top of the class.

Programs/ Assemblies/Extra Curricular Activities

Johnson School received a grant to host an after school program called Creative Afterschool Program. (CAP). Students attended CAP after the school day ended. They were given a snack, did homework, played games, and had physical activity on the playground. Some of their parents worked until five or six o'clock and needed CAP. Other parents chose to have their children stay after school as the charge was minimal. This program was well attended.

* * *

The Greater Lexington Chamber of Commerce began A.P.P.L.E. (Alliance of Programs and Partnerships for Lexington Education) in 1984. This was a joint effort between Fayette County Public Schools and the Greater Lexington Chamber of Commerce. The goal was to establish and cultivate partnerships among private sector businesses and education institutions in the county. The partners were committed to improving the education of Johnson students through shared resources

During the 1986-87 school year, the Lexington Philharmonic was our A.P.P.L.E. partner. Its annual booklet dedicated two pages to Johnson School's partnership with them. Our students enjoyed visits throughout the school year from the conductor who demonstrated the "art of conducting." Several touring ensembles, the Brass Quintet, Woodwind Quintet, and String Quintet also visited the school. Several of the students attended concerts off campus. One of the favorite performers was a classical pianist, Leon Bates, (real name) who played the piano for our students. He talked to them about staying in school and getting a good education while pursuing their talent. Students asked him questions and wanted his autograph!

Some of the members of the Lexington Philharmonic visited the school, ate lunch with the students, sat with the students during the Thanksgiving dinner, and came to our Christmas program. They were impressed with the students' interest in the orchestra and in learning to play the different kinds of instruments.

For a few years, Hillenmeyer Nurseries was our A.P.P.L.E partner. Some of the classrooms had field trips to the nursery to learn seed development, soil conservation, and how important trees are to the environment. Students received a flower seedling to grow in class. Horticulturalists spoke to many classes and made presentations about environmental education. The science teachers were given plants from the nursery for science experiments.

The A.P.P.LE. program benefited Johnson students and staff. Learning from different businesses exposed the students to a new and exciting view of Lexington, along with many future job possibilities for students when they were older.

* * *

One of the most popular programs for the fifth graders was the "Buddy Program". A professor at the University of Kentucky taught a course in "Public Speaking" which included the "Buddy Program". Through this program, female and male athletes in a U.K. class visited some of the local elementary schools, one of which was Johnson.

Over several years, different athletes visited the fifth grade classes. They talked to them about the importance of an education, and how their own good grades and athletic talent got them scholarships to the University of Kentucky. When some of the basketball players in the class visited our school, all the students were in awe of their size thirteen shoes and six foot seven inch frames. Students touched the players' arms and gazed up at them in admiration. One of our students asked a player to pick him up to see if his head touched the ceiling. When it did, the students clapped and cheered! The fifth grade boy was very impressed that the basketball player raised him up over his head so effortlessly. Each athlete had a "buddy " in the fifth grade. When time allowed, the "buddy" ate lunch with the student and observed him or her in class.

Our students enjoyed the athletes anytime they came to Johnson. However, the majority of our students didn't attend any basketball games at Rupp Arena (downtown) because they couldn't afford tickets. Many extra curricular activities and programs cost too much for the families to afford.

* * *

In the fall of every year, the Boy Scouts of America had their annual night enrollment for our third, fourth, and fifth grade boys. Many of the boys wanted to participate, but most of our students could not afford to join or buy a uniform. The representative from the Boy Scouts said there were scholarships available for a few boys but not as many as we needed. Additionally, the parents had to be involved. Several boys who showed up without a parent had to leave. It is a fine organization and the few boys who received scholarships really enjoyed the scouting activities.

One year a Johnson mother started a Girl Scout troop at the school. There were four girls in the troop. It was discontinued after one semester due to lack of funds and parental support.

* * *

One of the most creative and innovative programs in Lexington was Boy's Ranch. It was an educational opportunity for fifth and sixth grade boys from low socio-economic backgrounds. When the students were accepted, they lived on the ranch from middle school through high school. Those who remained in the program received college scholarships.

Boy's Ranch was funded by Anita Madden (real name), a local businesswoman and socialite, who made sure the boys were exposed to a well-rounded academic education. Farming duties, tutoring programs, most of the sports activities at the University of Kentucky, along with the arts and cultural events were a part of their education, too. Most Johnson students who applied were accepted. All of them went on to college or a university. Some of the teachers and I were invited to the Ranch to visit and eat dinner with the boys. Sometimes they came to school to visit. We were so proud of them! Thank you, Anita Madden.

* * *

Transylvania provided a mentoring program for our fifth graders one semester. A professor there had his class of thirty students be mentors to thirty Johnson fifth graders. (The students involved had parental permission).

The mentors came after school one day a week. The Transylvania students took our students on a visit to campus to see the dormitories, cafeteria, and gymnasium. Sometimes the mentors helped their mentees with homework after school. Some mentors visited the students' homes. A few of the mentors took students to basketball games or other activities on the Transylvania campus. After one of the Johnson students returned from the women's dormitory, she said to me in the office, "Miss Show, college girls act just like me. They watch T.V. together just like I do with my friends. I want to go to college when I get out of high school."

* * *

All schools in Fayette county celebrated "Public Education Day." Everyone in the community was invited to visit the schools from 9:00a.m.-6:00p.m that day. The Family Resource Center provided guest readers for the classrooms. Many parents visited their child's class on that day.

We invited central office staff and Fayette County Public School Board members to visit Johnson School whenever possible. One board member who visited our school was very impressed. It was crucial for the Board to visit because they enacted policies that affected all schools. Board members who visited schools helped them see similarities and differences in each one.

Once, during "Public Education Day," (it was announced outside on the marquee), the custodian came into my office and said, "There are two prostitutes who walked into our school and went straight to the bathroom. I won't clean in there if they use it and get their germs on everything."

I told him I'd take care of the situation. I walked down the hall into the girls' bathroom. The women were wearing full length leather coats and standing near one of the sinks. "Welcome to Johnson School," I said. "Would you like a tour of the building?"

One replied, "No, we already know what the school looks like." They exited the bathroom, walked down the hall, looked out the front door before leaving, then hurriedly ran in the opposite direction from the street corner. I had a gut feeling something wasn't right. I called the police and told them what had happened at school. The girls were picked up later in the morning. After school that day, one of the police officers came by Johnson to tell me the girls had stolen the leather coats from a nearby store.

The custodian sprayed the bathroom, washed down the walls, sinks, commodes, and anything else the girls could have touched.

* * *

Every year we celebrated "Unity Day" where all the students participated in a Unity Program in the gymnasium. We celebrated different cultures around the world through singing and performances. We all joined hands and talked about unity in different countries.

Unity Day was displayed on the outside marquee inviting parents and visitors to see the program. One of the people in the community came into the office waving a paper. She looked at me and said, "Pay this."

Confused, I asked, "What is it?"

She said, "My utility bill. Pay it. It says out there on that sign it's Utility Day."

"No, it is Unity Day."

She said, "What in the hell is Unity Day?"

"It is a time for all cultures to join together and help one another around the world." I replied.

"So, pay my bill," she said.

I firmly said, "I will not pay your utility bill." She stormed out of the office while mumbling a few choice words as she went through the front door.

* * *

Our fifth graders enjoyed the "Be Your Best Self " program which was sponsored by Kentucky Junior Miss participants. The high school girls were winners of The Kentucky Junior Miss pageant in their counties. The Junior Miss contest was based on intellect, talent, and beauty. Scholarships and opportunities for statewide appearances were awarded to the winner of the Junior Miss Pageant in Lexington.

The pageant committee had chosen Johnson School as a community service project for each contestant. They arrived at Johnson with big boxes of school supplies, clothing, dental products, soap, and a few educational games. The supplies were stored in the Family Resource Center and given out as needed to our children.

The contestants talked to all of the fifth grades about having healthy self-esteem, being proud of who they were, and the importance of a high school and college education. The girls were good role models for all the fifth grade students. There was a question and answer session afterward. (They thought my students would ask questions about the contest). One of the fifth grade girls asked, "Were you ever afraid of drive-by shootings?"

130

Several of the contestants said they had never seen one but a sharp girl said, "I know I would have been scared if gunshots were heard near my house." After their visit, the students wrote about the experience with the high school girls. A special thanks to the Junior Miss contestants.

* * *

Throughout each school year several teachers had mentoring programs. The programs involved visits from well dressed, professional businessmen who talked to the students. The visitors also taught different subjects to various grades.

During an economics session for the fifth grade, the guest speaker, a local banker, brought each student a checkbook. He taught them how to use the checking system at the bank. He put a thousand dollar "payroll" check in each student's hand and showed them how to deposit it in the bank. He showed them how to write checks for "rent," and balance their checkbooks. The banker told them about savings accounts and how important it was to save money each month.

One of the students asked, "Why can't welfare checks be deposited in the bank?" He had seen that government welfare checks had to be cashed and bills paid with cash. Food stamps were another topic of discussion. Why couldn't food stamps be deposited and checks written? Good questions!

"Where does the money come from for welfare checks since they aren't payroll checks?" The banker explained, "In America, paychecks for working class people have money deducted from them to pay for welfare checks for non-working people."

The light bulb went off. "I didn't know that!" One student said.

Another one asked, "Do you mean teachers and other people who work and get a paycheck have to give some of their money to people who don't work?"

"Yes," he said.

"Do principals have money taken from their paychecks, too?" One student asked.

"Yes."

"That isn't fair!" one student said.

Much discussion followed.

* * *

Many African American and white businessmen visited the students at Johnson and were invited to speak to all grade levels. It was important that the students saw men dressed for work in a suit and tie. They heard the visitors talk about the importance of staying in school and getting a good education.

When some of the local Urban County Government Council members ate lunch with the fifth graders, the students asked them to stop the shootings in the area and keep the neighborhood safe. The councilmen were dumbfounded; they had no idea the challenges that some of our students faced everyday, living in an inner city neighborhood.

* * *

The Parent/Teacher Association (formerly PTO-Parent/Teacher Organization) held meetings at the school, every month, in the evening. Students sang, played instruments or performed in a play for the parents.

Neighborhood associations held evening meetings at Johnson school, along with our district councilman because it was a safe place. I was present for all of the neighborhood and city council meetings. I felt my presence was important as a "community leader" and principal.

In 1994, the Mayor's office held several "Speak Out Lexington" meetings throughout the city in January and February. The citizens of every community came together and shared their opinions, concerns, and ideas about each neighborhood area. The results were then analyzed from all the meetings and the report was shared with the city council. This process was supposed to give new direction to them on new programs and policy decisions.

One of the "Speak Out Lexington" evening meetings was held at Johnson School. It was packed to capacity with concerned citizens from the community. Many senior citizens and parents were present. The panel was made up of the chief of police, the district councilman, a representative from the Mayor's Office, and a mediation person (he was in charge of the meeting, and listed the issues on a large chart for all of us to see). The issues from our area were:

- Gang activity in the neighborhood
- Prostitution on the streets during the day and night
- Thirteen bars in the community and drunks on the streets
- Sewer problems and flooded streets due to poor drainage
- Safety on the streets- several senior citizens had been mugged
- safe housing conditions, especially rental property

- Increased homeless population on the streets

There were no solutions or ideas offered for any of the problems listed above. We were told that the Mayor's Office would have a report on the issues over the next several months. It was a productive meeting in the sense that the people let the city leaders know their concerns.

However, the problems listed by the people in the community were there long before I arrived as Johnson's principal. Ironically, they were the same problems that I directly and indirectly faced during the sixteen years I was at Johnson. There had been little to no improvements in the identified concerns when I retired in 2001. In my opinion, the problems in a poor community, with senior citizens, the working poor, and welfare recipients, fell on the deaf ears of leaders downtown who could make a difference.

* * *

SCAPA (School for the Creative And Performing Arts) which was located in the former Bluegrass School building, in Lexington, Kentucky, performed for Johnson's second through fifth grades often over the years. Many of the teachers at SCAPA were talented in the fields of art, music, and drama as well as in academics. The SCAPA students performed these arts at school. Their shows also featured talented musicians and actors. They were well received at Johnson because we also had so many talented students in art, music, and dance. Many of our students had beautiful voices and sang in the school choir. Several students auditioned and performed in the Lexington Ballet's "Nutcracker." The students also played in the band and orchestra in the fourth and fifth grades. It was evident that parental support improved the arts education of these students.

SCAPA students motivated our students to be the best at whatever art form they enjoyed. When some of our students applied for SCAPA at the end of the year, a few were accepted. We were sad to see them leave Johnson School but were happy for their success. As the leader of the school, I promoted broad exposure to the arts as a career path in life for our students.

* * *

School assemblies featuring guest speakers, broadened our students' knowledge by exposing them to a much larger information world.

One of the most unusual assembly programs was given by a lady who traveled through various states talking about endangered raptors. She was certified to keep raptors which were injured and couldn't be released into the wild again. Our students and staff had never seen an American Eagle up close. She told us that the eagle had been shot, operated on, and healed. However, it could not fly in the wild again. She told the students to avoid ever hurting birds of any species. The eagle flew up to the far basketball goal in the gym on command. What a beautiful sight! As he flew back to his perch, we were in awe. She had different species of raptors but the eagle was the highlight. Some of our students were so impressed that they wanted to be bird handlers when they grew up!

* * *

One of our guest speakers was a descendent of a "Buffalo Soldier." Both students and parents were invited to this assembly. He told us that several freed black slaves went west with different Indian tribes before the Civil War. Dressed in a Civil War uniform, he had a musket, long knife, and buffalo skin. He said his great grandfather was a "buffalo Soldier" who rode with a number of Indians and helped win the Civil War of 1860. The name "Buffalo Soldier" came from the Indians who believed that the black soldier's hair was similar to buffalo fur.

"The "Buffalo Soldiers" played a very important role in the Civil War, and thus, should be in all United States history books," he said. The students asked many questions at the end of the assembly and all wanted his autograph! After the assembly, a student said she was related to him because he looked exactly like her grandfather.

* * *

The Junior League of Lexington performed a puppet show for third graders called "Kids On The Block." Some of the puppets had handicaps and talked openly about their disabilities. This talented group of puppeteers taught tolerance and understanding of children with disabilities. The students learned to be sensitive to the needs of others and to treat them with respect.

* * *

Before the Christmas holidays, during the 1980's-1990's, the Lexington Parks and Recreation Department brought the "Christmas Caravan" to Johnson School. The Caravan picked up canned goods that our students brought from home for needy families. In return, they performed for the students.

The dancers dressed in red and green outfits and danced to lively holiday music. Some of the University of Kentucky cheerleaders and the mascot did cheers and danced. There were clowns who made us laugh. "Smokey" the Bear was there and pretty girls in princess dresses sang. Rudolph pranced through the door with Santa Claus behind him yelling "Merry Christmas!" Mrs. Claus waved and smiled. The students cheered.

* * *

Assemblies were an important part of the students' school year. When folk and country dances were taught by the music and physical education teachers, we celebrated with country/western day. All the students and staff dressed up in boots, shirts, jeans, hats, and bandanas. Each grade level performed cultural folk/square dances that they learned, in an assembly for the parents and guests. The staff danced with some of the students as well as the parents!

The Johnson School Band/Orchestra performed in schoolwide assemblies twice a year. The chorus often sang in the school assemblies. During the holidays, the chorus sang at businesses, nursing homes, and other schools.

* * *

Every year before the Christmas holidays, Bank I sent Santa Claus to Johnson. He gave every student a gift. Thank you Bank I!

Fun Times with the Students

I thoroughly enjoyed being the Principal of Johnson School. I visited all of the classrooms and observed outstanding teaching in every grade level. It was a joy to observe students actively involved in the learning process, especially reading and math.

In the primary classrooms, I sat on the floor in a circle and had students read to me. They were excited to read the stories simply because they could! Some students read with great drama and wide arm gestures to accompany the words. The facial expressions of some of the readers made me think of actors in movies, giving wonderful presentations while spouting words into complete sentences. A few students, after reading to me, would explain the story with the different characters in case I didn't understand the gist of the plot!

In the Educable/Behavioral/Disturbed class, each student verbally shared life events of the night before or from the week-end. It gave the student an opportunity to talk about the circumstances of life experiences without screaming or fighting. The teacher and assistant were good at listening to the students and giving sound advice on alternatives to anger.

When math time came, students in the regular classes eagerly displayed their skills at the chalkboard or on paper. (Marker boards were in a few classrooms.)

When third through fifth grades had multiplication in math, I challenged each student to stand in front of the class, and recite the multiplication tables two through twelve without making a mistake. The reward was a five dollar bill which was taped on the blackboard.

"All you have to do is memorize the multiplication tables. Once you learn them, you'll know them for the rest of your life. You must know them to do division," I explained.

I gladly gave out many five dollar bills (out of pocket) to intermediate students for learning multiplication tables. Five dollars was a good motivator and was money well spent.

When a student correctly recited the multiplication tables, I gave the five dollar bill to him immediately. Everyone clapped for the student. The competition for winning the money spanned two weeks. Parents received letters or phone calls celebrating their child's success.

Before dismissal, at the end of the school day, the multiplication winners were announced. It was important to recognize the students academically as often as possible.

* * *

If you want to be a principal, know that in order for you to be effective in your school, you must be involved in it. This means being aware of what the students are learning and doing in their classrooms everyday. Walk the halls. Be approachable to staff and students. Make the time!

Being visible at breakfast and lunch were also very important to me. I often ate with the students. They enjoyed my presence and I enjoyed hearing their life stories.

* * *

A fun spring activity that I enjoyed with all grade levels was finding four leaf clovers on the playground during recess. Our playground grass had clumps of four leaf clovers. When I found one, I knew I'd find many more.

" I challenge any student who is not playing on the equipment or playing ball, to find four leaf clovers during your recess time."

"These are all three leaf clovers," one student said.

"Here is a four leaf that I found, just now," I countered. Some of the students were skeptical.

"There aren't any here," they said.

"Yes, there are. If you find one during your recess, and bring it to me, you'll get a dollar bill. The challenge ends after recess," I said.

The next thing I saw was students running around in the grass, dropping to their hands and knees, looking for four leaf clovers.

In ten minutes of physical activity, three students found four leaf clovers. I gave each of them one dollar.

However, with spit, one student broke a clover petal off and tried to make a fourth on a three leaf clover. One student split a clover and said it had four leaves. It didn't work. The other students reported that they cheated. It was a good lesson when peers took charge.

I kept the four leaf clovers in a cup on my desk for everyone to see. Later, several parents told me their children had them out in their yards at home looking for four leaf clovers!

* * *

One afternoon, the kindergarten class came to the gymnasium for their scheduled physical education class. The physical education teacher had not returned from a fifth grade field trip he was chaperoning so there was no teacher. Knowing it was the teacher's planning time, I told her I would teach the class so that she could have her 30 minutes of planning.

In my suit and heels, I led eighteen five-year old students into the gymnasium. The students warmed up by running from one end of the gym to the other. I noticed twelve bags of donated clothes sitting on the stage. I put six students in three groups while they sat on the floor.

"Today is your lucky day. We are going to play dress up," I said.

"How do you play that?" one student asked.

"Remember how you pretend to cook food in your classroom kitchen? Dress up is like that," I said.

Four donated bags of clothing were given to each group.

"You will all open the bags and put on any outfit you want. "

It was a sight to see! The students giggled and squealed as they put on adult vests, shirts, pants, skirts, jackets, and even a few ties. Some of the girls found dresses, hats, and dress gloves.

After everyone was "dressed up," we formed a line, and paraded out of the gym and into the main office. After the "oohs" and "ahhhs" of office workers, we paraded down the hall into a third grade classroom where the students clapped as we walked around. The kindergartners were proud of their outfits. One of the third graders said, "I've never played that game in my life. When do WE get to play it?" Good question.

We returned to the gym, put the clothes into the bags, and talked about our experience. I thanked them for having a fun time together. When their teacher returned they excitedly told her about the "dress up" game.

*　*　*

When I was a young girl, my middle sister and I played "dress up" in some of my grandmother's old clothes. We wore a vintage opera cape, the petticoat to her wedding dress, white gloves, and feathered hats. A real delight was wearing an old torn sealskin fur coat left over from the 1920's era. We had opera glasses and mother's high heels. What fun we had pretending to be at the opera or a tea party.

Nannie (grandmother) played classical music on the Acrosonic piano. My sister and I loved to sing "la la" to the music since there were no words to "Claire De Lune."

Sometimes my sister and I dressed Nannie up. She wore no corset so we put one of mother's bras on her for an "uplift." We squeezed her body into one of mother's dresses to go with the opera cape.

Nannie had beautiful long white hair. We styled it on top of her head with curls in the back which were held together by hair pins. The rouge and lipstick were applied last before she saw herself in the maple dresser mirror.

Nannie laughed at her vision of loveliness and we did, too. She was such a good sport to tolerate our "creativity" on rainy days when we couldn't play outside. I had a wonderful childhood.

The Principal and the Prostitute

Teeny Merritt was one of my favorite parents. I had never known anyone like her. She was very honest about her life and told it like it was.

Her son Tommy was in the third grade at Johnson. She worked the "stroll" at night and on the corners of Sixth Street and Limestone, everyday. (This was before the Safe School Zone was implemented).

Teeny was a petite, pretty girl with black hair and blue eyes. She occasionally sported a black eye and cut lip from being beaten by a "john."

One time, when she walked Tommy to school, I asked, "Teeny, why don't you come in and get your high school diploma? We're offering classes in the afternoon."

She looked at me and said, "Now Miss Show, you know I make more money out here in one week-end than you make all month."

I answered, "That's true, Teeny, but your looks are going to fade one of these days where as you could have a diploma for the rest of your life." She laughed and said, "Thanks anyway."

One time when Tommy hadn't been to school for three days, I made a home visit to Teeny's house. Teeny was passed out in the front yard. Alarmed I asked, "Teeny, where is Tommy?" I shook her shoulder until she looked up at me.

"At my mother's," she said.

I said, "He hasn't been to school in three days."

She said, "Damn it. She was supposed to take him to school."

I said, "Get yourself together and come to the school so we can talk."

Teeny cleaned up. She called her mother on the pay phone and told her to bring Tommy to school.

While she was in my office, waiting on her mother to bring Tommy to school, I said, "Teeny, why don't you get off the street? You're young and smart. You could get a job. There are resources for you to go to school. Tommy needs a stable mother."

"Aw, Miss Show, this is the only life I know. Mom had me doin' blow jobs when I was five years old. I don't know nothin' else."

It was then that I noticed needle marks on Teeny's arm and said, "Teeny, what are these marks?"

She said, "Oh, a john put them there. I'm no junkie."

When Tommy came to school, and Teeny left, I called Tommy's social worker about my concerns. I asked her to please make a home visit to check on Tommy.

He was eventually removed from Teeny because she was arrested with a "john" who had cocaine in his possession.

Tommy was put in the care of Teeny's mother. I protested but couldn't prove the story that Teeny told me. I didn't see Teeny on the street for ten years.

Teeny showed up one day with grown up Tommy and her new biracial baby. Tommy was in the service and on leave. I was glad to see them. "I've missed seeing you all. How have you been?"

Teeny said, "I was in prison in Alabama. The "john" I was with had a bunch of drugs and I was arrested, too. I've been there all this time. My baby's daddy is a prison guard down there. I didn't know I could get "knocked up" again. Big surprise. Do you still have clothes here?"

"Sure," I said, and had a parent volunteer take her to get clothes. Tommy looked at me and said, "She hasn't changed. She still hits the bars at night and gives the baby to anyone to watch. I'm glad I don't live here anymore. I have a girlfriend in another county and I stay with her when I'm on leave." I hugged him before he left and wished Teeny well.

Abuse

My early years as principal were busy years spent learning all the duties and responsibilities of the position. I was in court often over abuse/neglect/truancy issues involving some of my students. Most of the time I didn't have to testify but had to appear in case there were questions about my written statement. The questions were about what I observed or knew and medical information I was able to provide were helpful.

It was heart wrenching to see evidence of physical abuse on young bodies. There were whelps on the backs and buttocks from belt marks, bruises on the arms and legs, cigarette burns on various parts of the body, and iron marks on arms, backs, or buttocks. One time, a broken bone was the result of abuse.

I soon realized that the needs of some of the families were great. Many of them had addictions. Marijuana, crack cocaine, and prescription drugs, mixed with alcohol, were the choices of a few addicted parents.

Huffing paint was common for a few children. I knew this because a student of mine came to school one morning with glazed eyes. He was lethargic and had a faint silver paint rim around his mouth from holding the bag too close to his lips. When the rescue squad came to the school and examined him, they called his mother to come to the school and take him home.

A few of the parents talked openly about needing help for their addiction. Some were in denial that they had a drug problem. One student brought marijuana "butts" to school in a plastic bag while begging us to help her mother stop smoking pot. Child Protective Services was called and an investigation conducted. Mother and the children moved to another county at the end of the month.

For "show and tell" one time, in the first grade, a student brought a "roach clip" and showed classmates how it held things when it was pinched together.

A few parents found money anyway they could to support their drug habit. A small percentage of the robberies, shootings, and prostitution listed in the newspaper involved my parents. Unfortunately, some of the children were physically and sexually abused. Child Protective Services was called when a child came to school with cuts, bruises or broken bones.

When the parent was prosecuted and found guilty in a court of law, the children were placed in foster care or with grandparents or other relatives. Sometimes the family was reunited after their parents served their jail sentences. State social workers were at our school weekly, visiting foster children and talking to students who were active cases for other reasons.

Johnson had several social workers who were working with three to five families at one time. There were many turnovers in social worker positions. The new social workers came to the school to get necessary background information on some of their cases. We worked well together because it helped the children.

One of our regular state social workers set up a visit with a mother in rehabilitation who hadn't seen her two daughters in four months. The social worker thought it would be nice if they visited each other in the main office. I agreed. The mother and social worker waited while the seven and nine year old girls came to the office. The girls hugged their mother and sat down on the chairs for a short visit. Ten minutes later, yelling and screaming erupted between the mother and girls.

The mother hit one of the daughters in the face . The other girl jumped on the mother and started pulling her hair. I ran out of my office and pulled the girl off of her mother. I put her in a safety hold on the floor. The social worker grabbed the mother and held on tight until she quit screaming and yelling at the girls. It was a free for all in every way.

The school guidance counselor arrived and took the youngest daughter who had been hit in the face to her office. I took the oldest daughter to my office to calm down.

She cried, "I hate my mom. She is so mean. I can't stand the sight of her."

"I think you're just upset at what happened. You care about your mother and are upset that she hurt your sister," I said.

"No, that isn't it. Mom let smelly old men mess with my sister and me when she was high. She even sold our clothes to get more drugs. I hate her," she said.

I put my arms around her and she burst out crying. I held her until the tears stopped. Later, I took her to the school guidance counselor who talked with both sisters.

We needed more support groups for children with anger issues. The counselor and social worker's days were full; more service personnel were needed.

* * *

In 1990, we were fortunate to have a half-day three and four year old program at Johnson Elementary. It served three year olds with special needs as well as all four year olds who qualified for free or reduced lunch.

At one o'clock in the afternoon, one of the four year olds was still waiting at the school to be picked up. His phone was disconnected and no emergency phone was listed. I drove him to the residence listed on his enrollment card. He wanted to open the door and go in but I held his little hand and knocked on the door. I wanted to talk to an adult.

After five minutes of heavy knocking and yelling his mother's name, the door opened. The marijuana smoke almost knocked me over. Four adults lay on the floor in a daze. The mother at the door was so stoned that she didn't recognize me. She could hardly stand up.

"Hey Baby, come to momma," she slurred to the four year old. He went into the house and I returned to school. I immediately called Crimes Against Children and told them my concern about leaving a child in danger. They made a home visit and removed the four year old , a two year old and an infant from the house. The children were safe, at last. Mother was admitted to a rehabilitation program.

* * *

One five year old girl, Sheila, who was in the Educable Mentally Handicapped class urinated on herself daily. She would not go to the bathroom like the other students no matter what the teacher did to help her. Frustrated, the teacher talked to the nurse about making a home visit. The school did not have a phone number and the student was out of district.

The nurse asked me to accompany her since the parents had never visited the school. They lived on Bourbon Street. The student had told me that she lived on Liquor Street.

We sat down in the living room. The mother was in her early twenties. The father was sixty years old. A preschooler was running around naked in the house. He stopped long enough to urinate in a cardboard box in the corner of the room. The father told us the plumbing was "broke" in the house and the kids had to use the box since there was no water in the commode. (Something was wrong with this picture).

We told them our concern about Sheila urinating on herself and not being potty trained. I said, "Sheila has to use the commode at school and you have to help us. Here is a week's worth of panties for her to wear to school. Please teach her not to urinate in her pants at home and we'll help her at school."

Mom said, "We'll try."

Dad didn't say a word. Then he changed the subject. He said, "This is my second family. I got grown kids in Clay County."

We thanked them and left. I didn't have a good feeling about the father. Intuition told me something wasn't right with this family. The mother didn't give me eye contact the whole time we were there. I returned to school and called social services. I asked if the family's file was still active?

"Yes," said the social worker.

I said, "Please send their social worker out to the house. The plumbing is broken and the kids are using a box for a commode."

"We were out there two weeks ago and everything was alright."

"Well, it isn't now. I suspect some kind of abuse is going on," I replied.

She then stated, "That can't be. The abused child was removed from the home and the parents are in counseling."

I was shocked. I didn't know about the other child in the home who had been removed. I alerted the teacher and nurse about the situation.

Sheila's teacher found a beautiful pink organdy dress with a pink satin bow around the waist in the donated clothes. She showed it to Sheila. Her eyes lit up as she jumped up and down. She put her face into the satin bow and hugged it to her chest. The teacher said, "Sheila, if you use the bathroom, and do not pee in your pants by 10:00 a.m. you can wear the pink dress all day, everyday."

It worked! Sheila used the bathroom with the rest of the girls and got to wear the pink dress everyday. Before dismissal each afternoon, the teacher took the dress off of Sheila and put her own clothes on to wear home. The teacher took the dress home and washed it when it got stained.

Shortly after the following week, the teacher called me to look at some marks on Sheila's chest. The nurse came with me. We took Sheila to the restroom. The teacher said, "When I took her top off to put on her dress, I saw these marks."

"I was a bad girl last night and had to take my licks," Sheila said. On her chest over each nipple was a cigarette burn. The teacher put the dress on Sheila and the nurse took her to treat her burns. I was livid.

I called the social worker and said, "If you don't have Sheila's father arrested now, I will have you arrested for not doing anything."

The father was arrested. Sheila was placed in foster care where she bonded with the foster mother and was adopted a year later. Sheila blossomed and began talking in complete sentences, smiling and playing with the other students. She learned to count to one hundred and could add and subtract in math. Sheila learned to spell her name, and new last name, and wrote it everywhere.

In the third grade, Sheila was mainstreamed into a regular classroom with certain times of the day spent in the resource room. Sheila was a very smart little girl who had been traumatized in her young life by her father.

* * *

One time a second grade student was sent to the office for misbehavior. After reading the teacher's report, and the student saying he misbehaved in class, I asked him what he felt his punishment should be (SAFE or no recess).

He said, "Don't do anything. The teacher has already pulled my ear and put me in my hall locker in front of the class."

I was appalled. He sat in the outer office while I called another student from the class with the counselor present. The student told us the same story about the teacher punishing the student.

The counselor called three other students out of the same class one at a time, and they all told the same story. They returned to class and I asked the teacher to see me on her planning time.

She came into my office and admitted she had pulled the student's ear in play. She said she also had accidentally pushed him into the locker and shut the locker door.

I told her, "You are to stop touching the students immediately. You are not to pull a child's ear and put him in a locker, closet, or anywhere. I've been to court over physical abuse of parents and now I find out that I have an abusive teacher on my staff. It has to stop now!

Her eyes glared at me, and she said, "You have no idea how bad these kids are. I have to discipline them to keep them straight."

I warned her, "If you so much as touch one of your students you will never teach here again. You had problems with the last principal about this issue. It stops now."

"You weren't supposed to know about my past. It was confidential," she yelled.

She stormed out of my office and didn't touch another student the rest of the year. At the end of the school year she retired. She signed on to substitute elsewhere in the county.

* * *

During one of the ARC meetings for Special Education class at school, Mrs. Bales, the parent, said, "Just 'cause my other three girls are in Special Education classes don't mean Geri is, too. The doctor told me her I.Q. was 98.6. That's almost 100 perfect." The teacher, facilitator, Learning/ Behavior/Developmental (LBD) Resource teacher, parent and I were present at the meeting.

"Mrs. Bales, that's why we are meeting. Geri's tests are here. We want to discuss them to find the best educational program to meet Geri's needs," I said.

Mrs. Bales replied, "When I was a kid I went to that retarded school that closed. I used to be retarded but I outgrew it."

I said, "Perhaps Geri will, too. That's why I'm glad to you are here to see the test results." The mother agreed with us about the necessary support for her daughter. Finally, Geri got the help she needed.

I hesitated to share the rest of the story dealing with this family. However, I want administrators to know what they may have to deal with in the principal's position. John Q. Public should know what I had to face and do to save the children.

The youngest daughter in the family was three years old. She attended the Family Care Center on Red Mile Road for special training and education. A special bus picked her up at the house and returned her home everyday.

The director of the Family Care Center called me one day after school started, with concerns about frequent urinary infections that the three year old was having. I told her we were concerned about two of the sisters having constant bladder infections.

However, the girls would not say anything to the nurse to confirm that someone was "bothering" them. The girls were taking proper medication to clear up the infections only to have them return the next month.

I said to the nurse, "I suspect the girls are being abused but can't prove it."

"I feel the same way," the nurse said. "The girls will not say anything. They are very shy and secretive."

The suspicion lingered. A break came one Monday morning. Six-year old Geri came to school crying and upset. "What's the matter, Geri?" I asked.

She sobbed, "My daddy hurt my mommy and he needs to go to jail."

I called the eight-year old sister into the office. "What happened at your house over the week-end?" I asked.

"Mom and Dad got in a fight and he gave her two black eyes. He should go to jail. Mom is hurting bad, " she sniffed. I consoled them as best I could and walked them to their classes.

Mrs. Bales and another parent came to the clothing center later in the day. Mrs. Bales had two black eyes and a cut lip. She said, "My 'ol man and me had a fight Saturday night." She had no teeth and her bruised jaw barely opened. She and the parent left soon afterwards. I returned to the office.

Geri came to the office after lunch complaining of a stomach ache. I said, "I saw your mother and was sad that she has a hurt face but she is going to be alright."

Geri wailed, "Daddy hurt mommy and has to go to jail." Geri told me that she was afraid that her mother would die. I reassured her that she would live.

"I hate daddy. He has to go to jail for hurting mommy," she kept saying.

"Geri, look at me. Has your daddy ever hurt you or your sisters?" I asked.

She mumbled, "He flirts with us."

"What does it mean when you say he flirts with you?"

"I can't tell," she said.

We were sitting on chairs facing each other. Putting her little hands in mine I said, "Geri, you are safe here. No one will hurt you. But in order to help you and your sisters, I have to know what it means when you say your daddy flirts with you all."

She looked at me with her big brown eyes. "Mommy says no telling. When we go in the bathroom we lock the door so daddy won't flirt with us. Daddy hurt mommy and has to go to jail."

I persisted, "Geri, if you and your sisters are hurting, we can make it go away so it won't ever happen again, but you have to talk to me. You are safe here. Please tell me who is hurting you girls and what it means when your daddy flirts with you."

Geri was silent for a while, then the dam broke. She squeezed my hand real tight and groaned, "Miss Show, flirt is when daddy takes his pee pee and puts it in my pee pee hole. And you know where you poo poo? He puts his pee pee there, too. But daddy hurt mommy and needs to be in jail."

I was horrified. I gave Geri a sucker and called Crimes Against Children. Thank goodness the "doll therapist" came to school within a few minutes. A woman officer brought dolls for the child. Geri showed us, with the dolls, what her daddy had done to her and her sisters.

He was arrested within the hour. The girls were placed in foster care. That afternoon, Mom went free. I was so upset afterwards that I went home and vented to a friend on the phone for an hour. The pain and suffering these children went through for years was unthinkable, yet their main concern was for their mother's welfare.

A few weeks later Mrs. Bales had the nerve to storm into my office. She yelled, "You have to find me a man. You put my 'ol man in jail and I need another one." I wanted to smash her face!

Instead, I said, "It ain't gonna happen. Now leave and don't return again." She stormed out of the office yelling a few curse words. Two months later she was evicted.

* * *

Timothy was a second grader who was very polite and made good grades. He was well liked by the staff and students. His mother was very supportive of him. She came to all the teacher conferences and school programs.

In the third grade he was a different child. His grades dropped below average and he didn't hand in homework assignments. The teacher talked to the mother over the concerns but little changed.

Timothy picked on some of the boys in class and made one boy cry. He came to the office with a misbehavior form from the teacher. I looked at him and said, "What happened to the Timothy who was well liked and made good grades?" He was silent. He had to apologize to the students. I talked to the class about being considerate and kind to each other. I then called his mother and she said she would talk to him.

The next week Timothy cornered a boy in the restroom and pulled on his penis. The boy ran screaming out of the restroom into the classroom. He told the teacher, through tears, what had happened. Tim was in the office again. "Tim, what's wrong? This isn't the Tim we had last year," I said.

That Timothy is dead. This is a different Timothy now." He wailed, head down, and slumped shoulders.

"Oh, no. This is the same Timothy I knew in second grade. This year it seems you are angry with the world. Talk to me, Tim," I said.

My mom's gonna' have a baby. Her boyfriend lives with us," he said.

"That's good news, isn't it?" I asked.

"No. I don't like her boyfriend."

"Why not?"

He stated, "I liked it better when it was just mother and me."

"Well, what you did to the student was wrong. You have no right to touch another student for any reason. First, you will apologize to the student. Then you will go to SAFE for the rest of the day. I said. "I'll talk to your mother about this incident so she'll talk with you when you get home today." No comment from Timothy. He left the office with his head hanging and slumped over, walking with a shuffle.

I made a home visit after lunch to Tim's home. They lived behind the school. A brown dog and a white dog were in the yard. They were friendly. I knocked on the door. Tim's mother opened the screen door. "Your dogs are nice and friendly," I said.

"Yeah, the brown one's called "Hash" and the white one's called "Coke."

I sat down on a chair in the living room and explained my concern over Timothy's behavior. The mother said, "I don't know why he's changed but he's acting bad at home, too."

Just then the boyfriend came out of the bedroom. He appeared to be in a daze; he was covered with tattoos on his arms and face. He mumbled a few words and walked out the front door. (Something wasn't right).

"Congratulations on your baby," I said.

"Thanks. He's the daddy, she replied. "He got out of prison this summer and we're makin' a new start."

"Is he Tim's father, too?" I asked.

"Oh no, I met him this summer," she said.

I returned to school and called social services. My "gut" feeling was that there was abuse in the family. I told them about the extreme change in Tim's behavior. Something wasn't right about the situation at home. They said they would come to school and talk to Timothy. They came before dismissal. I called Timothy to the office and introduced him to them.

"They want to ask you some questions, Tim," I said. He grabbed my arm and said," I want Miss Show to stay with me."

Tim held onto my arm through the questions of possible abuse. He buried his face in my arm and turned his head to peep over at the social worker.

"I hate mom's boyfriend. He plays in bed with mom then makes her get out. Then he makes me get in bed with him." Timothy buried his head in my arm to hide the tears.

"He makes me put my mouth on his private parts and he does it to me."

Timothy was crying hard as I put my arms around his small body. I said, "Timothy, you are safe. No one will hurt you again."

He cried, "I told mom but she said I was lying. She said he gives us money to buy a lot of stuff. I don't like him. He scares me!"

The boyfriend was arrested later that day. Timothy was placed in foster care with a foster father. Tim's mother was furious that Tim had told a "big lie."

Over the years Timothy and the foster father visited the teachers and me. When Timothy was twelve years old he was adopted by the foster father.

Tim stopped by Johnson when he was a senior in high school. He told us about the college he was going to attend the following year. He had grown into a fine young man with a big smile on his face. This journey through childhood with his foster father was a happy ending for Timothy.

* * *

Tessa was in the morning kindergarten class. She was a real concern to the teacher because she constantly played with her private area. She wore dresses all the time. She kept her hands in her panties, fondling herself.

In the beginning the teacher tried to ignore her behavior. She redirected Tessa by giving her additional work to keep her hands busy. She had Tessa wash her hands often because there were "hands on" books and toys which all the students used daily.

Problems with Tessa touching herself worsened. The other children didn't want to be around her. I finally made a home visit and told the mother to have Tessa wear pants to school. The father was there, too. He had a tattoo on his right knuckles that spelled L-O-V-E and on his left knuckles were the letters H-A-T-E.

Curious, I asked, "What do the words mean?"

He said, "Where I come from these tattoos tell people we take care of our own, not the law."

I thanked them for the visit and returned to school.

Tessa was very intelligent for a five–year old. She finished her work before the other students were half way through their own. Waiting on the rest of the class to finish gave her time to scoot her bottom back and forth in her chair, while trying to get her hands into her pants. The teacher kept her working on projects to keep her hands occupied.

The final straw with Tessa was at restroom break. A boy in the restroom ran into the hall where the teacher was helping another student put her art work on the wall. (The assistant was in the room with the rest of the students).

He screamed, "Tessa's in the bathroom. She grabbed my pee pee. It hurts!" The teacher ran into the bathroom and got Tessa. She was sent to the office.

"How did you get into the boys' bathroom?" I asked.

"I went in there when the teacher wasn't looking."

I called Tessa's mother. I told her I was bringing Tessa home and needed to talk to her. When we arrived at Tessa's home, I told the mother what had happened at school. The mother said, "Oh, Tessa needs her "twatty" cream. Go get it girl so I can put some on you." I was shocked but didn't say anything. I didn't know what to say.

"Tessa has a rash down there and she takes medication for it." The mother said.

Tessa returned, gave her mother a big tube of cream, took her pants and underwear off in front of us, laid down on the floor, and spread her legs apart. Her mother applied the cream on her red genitals. Mother said nonchalantly, "Tessa had a rash for a while but the doctor said it was getting better."

I could hardly believe what I had witnessed. I said goodbye to them, returned to school, and called social services about the home visit. They made a home visit and found no one at home. When Tessa came to school the next day, the school social worker asked Tessa about her rash. She said her father gave it to her.

"I told daddy I didn't want him in my bed at night."

The doll therapist from Crimes Against Children came to the school. Tessa showed them what her father had done to her. Tessa was put into foster care and the father was arrested. The mother went to court and told the judge that she and I must be sisters because we looked alike. She also said that she felt we were conspiring against her and her husband. The mother threatened to bring a gun to school and shoot me for having her husband arrested and her child removed. A person from the court called me at school. She said to lock the school doors because the mother had threatened to shoot me.

I locked the doors and swore out a warrant for the mother's arrest. No one had the right to threaten me at school nor put the staff and students in harm's way.

The mother couldn't make bail so she spent the week-end in jail. The school doors remained locked.

Several days later some of the neighbors showed me a letter that had been left on several peoples' doorsteps. It said that I was a child abductor who stole children away from their parents.

The police made a home visit and warned Tessa's mother to stop making threats. She moved a week later.

Thirteen years later, grown up Tessa came to Johnson after school to pick up two boys she babysat. I was glad to see her. I asked, "Tessa, did we do the right thing by having you removed from your home?"

She looked at me and said, "Yes. The first foster home wasn't good, but the second one was great. My father had abused me since I was a little girl. They are divorced now. Mom had a heart attack and lives on Limestone Street. She'd love to see you."

I made a home visit to the mother's apartment the following week. She had aged twenty years and had an oxygen tube running into her nose. The mother apologized to me and said, "Let's be friends." I hugged her and didn't visit her again.

50<u>th</u> Year and 100<u>th</u> Year Celebrations

In 1989, we had two celebrations. One celebrated the original Johnson School which had been built on Fourth Street 100 years ago. The second celebration recognized the present Johnson School which had been on Sixth Street for 50 years.

The original Johnson Elementary, on Fourth Street, was for white children. It was named for Lexington Mayor Clyde Johnson who proposed a bond issue in 1887 to relieve overcrowded schools. The school was finished in November 1888 and was located at the corner of Fourth and Limestone Streets. Russell Elementary School, on Fifth Street, was the school for colored children and was one block away.

Mrs. Emma Price, a lovely black lady who lived across the street from the present Johnson School told me, "When I was a little girl I lived on Fourth Street and had to walk past Johnson School for white people and walk to Russell School for colored people on Fifth Street. There were times in the winter when I wanted to stop at Johnson and go to school because I was so cold."

The big houses in the area were one family residences. Many Transylvania staff, and prominent business people lived in them.

According to Mrs. Price, wealthy black families lived on Chestnut, Maple and Ohio Streets. The first "colored" subdivision was located at Illinois and Kinkead Streets. (It was later demolished to create the Rose Street Extension up to Sixth Street).

The African Cemetery #2, on Seventh Street, has many famous black people buried there. Race Street had the first race track in Lexington where several famous black jockeys won races during that time. They are buried with doctors, lawyers, and other prominent black people from the early years in the Seventh Street Cemetery.

In 1938, plans for a bigger Johnson School at the present site on Sixth Street began. Oram Florist owned green houses located on Sixth Street. They sold the land for the new school that was completed in 1939.

Businessman "Boots" Bramlett told me, I remember carrying my school books from Johnson School on Fourth Street to the new Johnson School on Sixth Street. It was an exciting time for us to go to the new school."

Over the years, the downtown people moved out to the suburbs. The large homes were remodeled into several apartments for working poor and welfare recipients. Low income housing was prominent in the area. Many downtown businesses moved out to the malls in the suburbs or closed.

By the time I became principal of Johnson School, in the 1985-1986 school year, the student population was 50% black and 50% white. Most of our families were transient. Several black grandparents who were raising their grandchildren owned their homes. Some of our white families were homeowners. However, the majority of our families rented and moved every few months or every year. Some families were evicted. After eviction, they moved to another low income area only to return to our area months later. Many of the residents who had attended one or both Johnson Schools still lived in and around the downtown area.

Announcement of the Johnson School 50th /100th Years Celebration Open House was on the marquee. The Open House was on flyers posted in local businesses throughout the neighborhood. It was spring. The front of the school was in bloom with green bushes and spring flowers.

Four students who attended the original Johnson School came to the Open House. The staff and I hugged them because they were still living! Johnson students escorted visitors through the school. Some of the former students of the existing Johnson School, who attended thirty years ago, didn't recognize the inside of the school. It was remodeled in 1955, 1958, and 1988. Many of these former students shared wonderful memories of their school years. The Johnson chorus sang. Punch and cookies were served in the gymnasium, afterwards. Friends were reunited and a good time was had by all. I was proud to be the principal of a school with so much history.

Johnson School in 1889

Johnson School in 1939

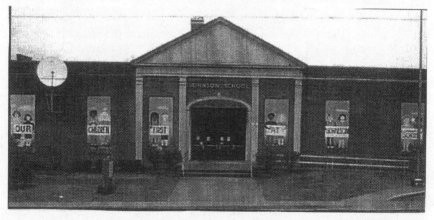

Johnson School in 2001

Mrs. Emma Price

One school year, during Field Day, the kindergartners were running races on the front side yard facing Sixth Street. I sat out front watching the five-years olds. I noticed an elderly lady sitting on her front porch across the street, also watching Field Day events.

"Hello!" I yelled. "Would you like to come over and join us?"

She replied, "I'd love to."

As she got up from her chair I noticed that she dragged her left leg as she walked. I crossed the street and helped her to the school yard where she sat down in a folding chair beside me.

"My name is Emma Price."

I introduced myself. We watched the races. When the students ran across the finish line they received their ribbons. They ran over to hug me and showed off their winnings. Since Mrs. Price was sitting there, they hugged her, too. When the races were over I thanked her for visiting us. She said, "I am the one who is thankful for being here. I haven't been hugged by anyone for a long, long time. Thank you, my dear."

In the early 1980's there were designated smoking areas in the school. Several teachers and I smoked. Later on, smoking was not allowed on school property. A few staff and I smoked across the street during their free lunch time or after school. Some of the best solutions to problems were discussed whiles smoking. That's the way it was. The problem with standing on the sidewalk to smoke was the "johns" who drove by, stopped their cars, and asked, "Are you available?"

We said, "No, we're just smoking."

Mrs. Price came to our rescue. On her porch across from the school, she said, "You girls come up here to smoke with me. They won't bother you up here." (She had a bench and chairs on the porch).

So began one of the most meaningful relationships of my career. I had in-depth conversations with a lovely, elderly black lady named Emma Price. She had lived in the neighborhood most of her childhood and adult life. For a few years she had lived in Ohio. She moved back to Lexington when her mother was ill. Emma was a widow whose twenty-year old son was killed in a car accident many years earlier. Her mother died and left her the house across the street from the school.

Dear Mrs. Emma Price was full of humor and history of Lexington. She loved a good drink occasionally. Our long talks were on Saturday when I took a break from all the school paperwork on my desk. Sometimes, after school, when everyone had vacated the building, I sat with Mrs. Price on her porch. I listened to wonderful stories about her childhood- some funny and some sad.

One day on the porch, Mrs. Price said, "My body doesn't work well on my left side because I had a stroke. You know, I laid there on the floor inside my door for three days before the mailman noticed me through the mail slot. I tried to yell at him but all that came out was a croak. The medics got me to the hospital but my left side was gone by then. I can't use my left arm and hand, and I have to drag my left leg around. I do alright for an old lady. My friend up the street I talk to, is in a wheelchair. I'm lucky."

When computers came to Johnson School, Mrs. Price came to my office one Saturday morning. She wanted to look at a computer and some of the software provided for the students. She was amazed at the different education programs.

"Mrs. Price, do you play solitaire?" I asked.

"I play it all the time," she said.

"Let me show you how to play it on the computer."

For the next two hours, with the mouse in her right hand, Mrs. Price played solitaire on the computer. She won most of the time. I took her picture and displayed it on the office bulletin board.

One Saturday Mrs. Price said, "You come to my house all the time. I'd like to go to your house sometime."

"Not only will you come to my house, you'll eat lunch and visit awhile. Where else would you like to go?" I said.

"In my young life, I went to Paris, Kentucky and partied on week-ends. It was a place to visit and stay with friends. I'd like to go there and see it again."

We made a date for "Emma's Day" one Saturday. I drove a used sports car when I didn't drive the van. I picked her up in it early on a Saturday morning. When she came out of the front door I noticed that she had painted her shoes brown. (She was given clothes out of our clothing center to keep warm but I forgot about the shoes). She felt she looked good and that was the important thing. It was a sunny spring day so I opened all the windows and sun-roof, and played Mrs. Emma's favorite jazz songs. She had a smile on her face all the way to Paris!

We drove around town looking for a street she knew sixty-five years ago. We stopped at a gas station to ask directions to the street location. The senior black gentleman sitting outside said, "That street isn't there anymore. The dance hall and houses are gone, too. If you go over the hill, and down by the curve in the road, you'll see where it used to be. It's mighty nice of you to want to find the street for her. Where you all from?"

We said Lexington, thanked him, and drove over the hill, to the curve in the road. We turned onto a dead end drive with trash and weeds on each side. I stopped the car. Mrs. Price said through watery eyes, "One time this place was hoppin' with a bar and dance floor over here. (her frail finger pointing to a slab foundation). I stayed in a house down the road. There were many good times I had here dancing, drinkin', and lovin' the night away!"

The gleam of excitement was in her eyes as she revisited memories of her younger days. We sat in the car for a long time; I drove slowly down the road, as she told stories of long ago.

Returning to Lexington, she wanted to visit an obscure cemetery behind Lexington Cemetery on Main Street. We drove onto a different street to get to Cove Haven Cemetery; she knew a lot of people buried there. We drove all over Lexington. She was shocked at how much the scenery had changed. (She had been to her doctor's office only. She hadn't seen downtown in twenty years).

At my home we had a late lunch. She walked through my house, then out into the back yard, where she told me the names of all the trees and shrubs. Mrs. Emma was full of knowledge about nature. She had so much common sense about life that never ceased to amaze me. While she talked I realized how fortunate I was to have such a lively, lovely senior friend.

One July afternoon Mrs. Price complained about her feet being sore. She said she could not walk in her shoes. Looking at her bare feet I saw that her toenails were overgrown which prevented her from wearing shoes correctly.

"Mrs. Price, your toenails need to be clipped." I said.

She replied, "I know but the doctor wants too much money to clip each toe."

I replied, "Tomorrow, I'll bring clippers and a file from home. I'll clip your toenails so that you can wear your shoes comfortably." There were tears in her eyes. "I used to clip my grandmother's toenails when she couldn't reach them. I'll do yours, too."

The next day, after work hours, I sat on Mrs. Price's porch. She was soaking her feet "to clean and soften the toenail for easy clipping." I towel dried her feet after I clipped her nails shorter so she could wear her shoes. Afterwards, she hugged me. I was overwhelmed at her gratitude. It was such a small favor to clip the nails of a disabled elderly person; it meant a great deal to her.

Several times in conversation with Mrs. Price, on her front porch, she talked about her "freedom papers." She said, "I have papers that prove I am a free person and not a slave. I can live anywhere I want to. I lived in Ohio 'til mother got sick and I had to come here. I can go anywhere and ride a bus or a taxi. I am free."

I didn't understand why that was so important to her until she told me stories about the injustices of her race in Lexington. There were no history books I had read, growing up in West Virginia, that talked about the plight of the black race. There were a few famous black people mentioned in the texts along with their contributions to society. Mrs. Price was my teacher and I was her student.

Several years later, Mrs. Price passed away at the age of eighty-seven. There were no relatives who came forward to make funeral arrangements so the city buried her in Cove Haven Cemetery. The house was gutted and all furniture and belongings were removed. I asked the cleaning crew to try and find Mrs. Price's "freedom papers." They did, a few days later. They found an old copy of The Emancipation Proclamation by Abraham Lincoln. I ran copies for all the classroom teachers to share with their students. This was a teachable moment for Johnson Elementary students. They knew Mrs. Price because she visited the school for special programs.

I was grateful to God for sending this wonderful person to me. Her words of wisdom and humor saw me through some challenging times as principal. She gave me good advice and guidance on many issues. I miss

Mrs. Price. The front porch bench is in my back yard. Family and friends enjoy sitting there. Thank you, Mrs. Emma Price!

Mrs. Price on her front porch

KERA (Kentucky Education Reform Act)

The Kentucky General Assembly and the Governor's Office formed a task force for educational reform in 1989. It had a huge impact on the academic future of Kentucky's children. KERA became law on July 13, 1990.

KERA mandated that every school in the state of Kentucky would be held accountable for the educational progress of its students. Grants to support schools in reaching high standards were made available.

In the fall of 1991, Johnson School was awarded a Family Resource Center. Applications were submitted to the state Cabinet for Human Resources from several elementary schools in Fayette County who had high percentages of free and reduced lunch students.

The Johnson Family Resource Center (FRC) was housed in the school. It had a coordinator and secretary. It impacted our families in many positive ways. It was open all year, thus, it was able to provide help for families during the summer when school was not in session.

If a student enrolled at Johnson School, the FRC provided school supplies, clothing, and support with other resources to help meet the family's needs. It also provided assistance to teachers with parent volunteers, extra school supplies when needed, and dry clothes for a student who had an "accident" in class.

The FRC was in charge of clothing donations which arrived weekly, from friends, teachers, bank employees, and local consignment shops. The custodian and I picked up many bags of clothing from these shops and delivered them to the school.

Parent volunteers sorted the donated clothes into storage bins for the students. When there was an abundance of donated clothes, the FRC held

Community Clothing Day in the gymnasium, for two hours. (There were no classes scheduled in the gym on Tuesday mornings).

The event was announced on our marquee in front of the school. Our parents, senior citizens, and other community people came to Clothing Day. The FRC and parent volunteers organized and monitored the event in the gym. It was a great public relations event. The community looked forward to it each month.

* * *

One Saturday morning, while driving to the inner city, a donated clothing incident occurred. It was 8:00 a.m. I was on my way to Johnson. I had twelve black leaf bags in the back of my van which were filled with donated clothes.

A police officer signaled me over to the curb. He and his partner cautiously walked up both sides of the van. He stopped at my window.

"May I see your license and registration?" he asked.

"Yes." I said." What's wrong?" Meanwhile the other officer was looking at all the bags in the van.

After he looked at my documents he said, "Your rear left tail light is out. It needs to be replaced."

"Thank you very much. I'll get it fixed," I said.

"Where are you headed?" He continued.

"I have bags of donated clothes for Johnson School."

The officers followed me to Johnson School on Sixth Street. They watched as I took the bags out of the van and carried them inside the school. Then the officers left.

I can only imagine how suspicious I looked with a van full of big black plastic bags in the inner city, early on a Saturday morning!

* * *

One year, in response to the needs of several high school students, the Johnson FRC collected evening gowns. A few weeks before the high school proms, several students were invited to the school to select a free gown of their choice.

A very popular activity that the FRC held with Johnson parents was craft night. FRC had guests who taught crafts to the parents and children which they completed together. Some of the instructors also taught academic activities which included homework strategies for interested parents.

Free computer classes for Johnson parents were another big hit. Parents learned how to use a computer, the internet, and several programs. Childcare was provided during class time.

The FRC hosted monthly parent support groups. Guest speakers discussed parental concerns and solutions to help them with their children. Lunch was provided. Since many of our students were being raised by grandparents and foster parents, there were also support groups for them.

Some of our grandparents enjoyed coming to the FRC everyday just to talk and visit. They also volunteered when needed. There were many resources such as pamphlets on various subjects, referrals for rent assistance, child care, clothing, cleaning supplies, and educational opportunities for the parents, grandparents, and foster parents. The FRC kept our families informed.

One of the favorite FRC family events was "Readyfest" which was held on the Saturday before the first day of the school year.

Food, drinks, and school supplies were given to the families who attended. Teachers were present to greet new students and their parents. Forms for free/reduced lunch, updated addresses, and Title I programs, were filled out and signed by the parents. (This eliminated long lines of parents waiting to enroll their children the first day of school).

One of the local service organizations hired a clown to make balloon animals for the children. Music played through speakers and face painting created a festive atmosphere. The DARE police officer, mounted police, and the local Fire Department participated by bringing horses and a fire truck to the event. Students got to see inside the fire truck and received hats to wear.

The event was well attended by our families, some of whom brought grandparents and cousins with them. The smell of grilled hot dogs permeated the street. Several homeless people were able to get a free meal as well.

The FRC worked collaboratively with Title I (federal school education support program). One year, when eight parents needed their G.E.D.s (General Education Diploma) to graduate from high school, the FRC brought in a G.E.D. instructor.

The class was held in an empty classroom in the afternoon before school was dismissed. A teacher from Fayette County Public Schools Title I department taught the class. The majority of the women passed the course and received their G.E.D.s.

A popular FRC event was the "Bring the Man in your Life to Breakfast" at Johnson. It was held in February each year. Students invited any man in their lives (father, grandfather, uncle, neighbor, or friend) to school to eat a hearty breakfast with them as a pre-Valentine Day celebration.

The cafeteria staff cooked a superb meal for all the guests and students. It consisted of eggs, bacon, ham, hot biscuits and gravy, baked sliced apples, hot coffee, milk, and juice. The FRC funded the event so it was free to all the visitors. Pictures were taken of the students and guests which were displayed on the school/community picture board in the main office.

In May, near Mother's Day, the FRC sponsored "Muffins with Moms" breakfast which was similar to "Man in your Life," where mothers, grandmothers, foster mothers, aunts, female neighbors, or female teachers and I (if a mother couldn't attend), ate breakfast with a student. The students loved to have their mother or other female adult eat breakfast with them. Their pictures were posted on the school and community picture board.

In the spring each year, the FRC sponsored a well attended "Community Baby Shower." It was held in the cafeteria after lunch but before school dismissal. Lots of baby clothes, diapers, strollers, car seats, and baby furniture were donated and collected throughout the year for the event. Parent volunteers put baby items in a storage unit at school until the day of the shower. The FRC had guest speakers who talked to the mothers-to-be about infant nutrition and good health during pregnancy. Brochures on pre-natal resources and infant services in Lexington were given to them.

Everyone who attended the shower received baby gifts, diapers, infant clothing, and baby furniture. (We had enough for every mother). It was so successful that we had two baby showers the following year!

One year, the FRC had monthly group meetings for older students whose parents were incarcerated. Several intermediate students (fourth-fifth graders) were interested in what parents did in prison everyday. Prison activities were explained by the prison warden or a local jail employee who were also guest speakers. A signed permission slip from the student's guardian or parent allowed the child to attend the monthly meetings. It was also a time when the students wrote letters to their incarcerated parents.

Another service the FRC provided was vouchers for free eye glasses for students who needed them. Bus tokens and taxi vouchers were available to families in an emergency or crisis.

The FRC gave family passes to the Children's Museum on Short Street, in downtown Lexington, along with the Living Arts and Science Center, when there were ticketed events. Many events were free and within walking distance of Johnson School.

The FRC also supplied books throughout the school year for students who achieved academically, improved their behavior, and/or attained perfect attendance.

Students who wanted to go to summer camp were provided scholarships by the YMCA and 4-H Clubs.

Many parents volunteered in the FRC. The mothers and grandmothers who volunteered often ate lunch with the FRC staff and enjoyed "girl talk." On occasion, I was able to eat lunch with them. I shared some of the concerns I had had with my own children.

"I didn't think you had problems like me," one mother said. "Thank you so much for sharing."

"I am a mother just like you; no matter how old I am or what my job is, I am still concerned about my children."

One mother was so excited about a new man in her life that she talked about him during lunch in the FRC. "He took me to a fancy restaurant. We had "advertisements" before we ate dinner. They were so good!" (She meant "appetizers") I was glad that she had a good time.

Many families received a donated turkey for Thanksgiving but didn't know how to cook it. Either they didn't have a big enough stove, their gas or electric was turned off, or there was no roasting pan. Some of the frozen turkeys were sold to others instead of being thawed and cooked.

Seeing this need, the FRC provided a class on how to cook a turkey dinner for the interested parents. Roasting pans were donated. Several mothers learned how to prepare a turkey and made side dishes to go with it. They were so excited about the class that on Thanksgiving Day, several of the families got together and cooked turkey dinner to share with each other.

A very popular event at the FRC was "Free Haircut Day." Five hair stylists donated four hours of their time, one Saturday, to cut students' hair. They were professional hair stylists who cut and styled both black and white childrens' hair. It was well received as eighty students left with new hair cuts.

For several years on Tuesdays, the FRC sponsored "Bread Day".

Volunteers from The faith community collected "day old bread" and brought it to the FRC each week. Bread, cakes, doughnuts, and rolls were donated from by a local grocery store chain. Bread Day was advertised on the marquee out in front of the school. The inner city community was invited to the school to select bread supplies during specific hours in the morning.

Students celebrated their "birthday month" in class with a donated cake from the FRC. It was a special treat for many of our students who didn't receive a cake for their birthdays. However, some parents were able to bring birthday cupcakes or cake to their child's classroom to celebrate birthdays. The FRC made sure that every child's birthday was recognized each year.

FRC volunteers helped make bulletin board displays for teachers, copied anything the teachers needed for the students, and helped in the library.

Working in the inner city opened my eyes to the challenges that educators faced everyday. Being in the principal's position, I was called the instructional leader, and manager of Johnson School. However, these titles were not as important as building relationships with the families of my students. Despite the fact that the school was there to educate the children, crises that the family experienced became my priority, sometimes, whether I liked it or not. Thank goodness, for the Family Resource Center.

* * *

In 1990 KERA opened many doors for Kentucky Schools to apply for grants that would enhance the academic success of their students. KERA motivated schools to discover what worked academically for their students. Johnson students improved drastically with every grant we were awarded. The new focus on testing outcomes, coupled with teachers learning new ways to teach core curriculum subjects, resulted in stronger academic approaches where areas of weakness had existed.

It took several years to build a dedicated, professional staff who wanted to stay at Johnson. Staying meant having annual training in all aspects of curriculum, classroom management, and technology skills. Every new program learned and applied in the classroom resulted in improved academic scores for our students.

* * *

Since Johnson School served a population of 96% of its students on free and reduced lunches, poverty was an ongoing problem for parents and children. In answer to the high numbers of children affected by the challenges of poverty, Fayette County Public Schools and "Head Start" teamed up to provide an all day program. "Early Start" was state funded and included four year olds and special needs three year olds who ate breakfast at school everyday, had classes and left at noon. Only a half-day program, we realized that the children needed more time at school than they were getting. Thus, we applied for, and received a grant for the "Blended Program." Early Start (state funded) was held in the morning and Head Start (federally funded) was held in the afternoon.

The Blended Program was a huge success! The students had breakfast followed by classroom activities for academics and socialization. They ate lunch, played outside, had naps, resumed academics, and ended with social skills. At the close of the school year they were prepared for kindergarten.

A teacher in the Blended Program expressed concern that the students would forget what they had learned the school year during the summer. So she wrote a grant to provide a Backpack Program during the summer. It was denied due to lack of funds. At the end of the school year, we revised the grant and received funding from the Cabinet for Families and Children.

Two parents were hired to fill the backpacks with books, school supplies, and activities for the three and four year olds to do at home with a parent. These parents delivered the backpacks to all of the students' homes every week. At the end of the week, the backpacks were returned to be refilled with new books and activities. Sometimes, I went to the homes with the two parents when they delivered the refilled backpacks. All of the parents enjoyed interacting with their children. I was pleased to hear the parents rave about the Backpack Program. If the student finished everything in the backpack before the end of the week, the parent could bring it to the school and get it refilled early. This program helped the students retain what they learned during the school year. They were ready for kindergarten the next August.

* * *

In the 1990-91 school year, all Fayette County elementary schools sixth grades were moved into newly formed middle schools. Students in middle schools were in grades six, seven, and eight. Ninth grades moved to high schools where they joined tenth, eleventh, and twelfth grades.

The following year, Johnson School implemented the SBDMC (Site Based Decision Making Council). It consisted of three teachers, two parents, and the principal. Our charge was to adopt policies relating to instructional materials, curriculum, extra-curriculum activities, personnel, and other areas of school management.

* * *

Due to the high percentage of free/reduced lunch students attending Johnson, the school qualified to be a Chapter I Schoolwide School. (Chapter I was changed to Title I in later years). Chapter I teachers who taught reading and math were able to have smaller classes which provided more individualized instruction in each grade level.

KERA was in all schools statewide. It was the most drastic educational reform in the nation. Teachers were trained in new ways of teaching and testing students.

The first state test was called KIRIS (Kentucky Informational Reading Inventory System). It was given to fourth and fifth graders in the spring of every year. Creating writing portfolios was every fourth grader's responsibility as they were a part of the state test.

When the first years' test scores were published, Johnson School's test scores were very low, especially the writing scores. Thus, we qualified for a writing grant. Over the next two years, an outstanding writing specialist trained our staff in writing strategies for the students. The staff and students benefited from her writing expertise as the writing portfolios improved the following year. Writing portfolios were started in kindergarten and continued through fifth grade. However, only fourth grade portfolios were included on the state test. By the time the kindergartners were in fourth grade, writing was a part of the curriculum. They had developed impressive writing portfolios. Many students became avid journal writers in their classes.

An important part of journal writing, that positively impacted the students, was the freedom to express fears, abuse, or suicidal thoughts. The staff read each student's writing, and reported any of the above concerns to the counselor, social worker, nurse, or principal. When appropriate, the Cabinet for Families and Children, or the police Crimes Against Children Unit was immediately notified.

Teacher training for components of KERA was an ongoing process every year because Johnson's test scores were very low both in the county and statewide. We wondered what we could do to improve the scores for the annual state test? Our students showed improvement academically with the curriculum we taught, but they did not have good test taking skills. The staff responded to this problem by becoming pro-active. They taught students how to prepare for, as well as take, the state test.

Charts were displayed all year in the fourth and fifth grades showing the four different levels of tested skills. The beginning level was novice. The next level, showing improvement, was apprentice. By the following spring, students were challenged to be at higher levels which were the proficient and distinguished categories. Teachers tested all skills levels on class tests throughout the year. When testing time came in the spring, our students were ready to demonstrate the testing strategies that they learned.

Once we received the results of the state test, we analyzed our strengths and weaknesses. We had training to improve the weaknesses in preparation for the upcoming year.

From 1991-93, our students showed little improvement on the Kentucky Informational Reading Inventory (KIRIS). One of the challenges to improving KIRIS scores was how to educate the transient students who enrolled at Johnson in April and May. They had minimal testing preparation along with partially completed writing portfolios. Another issue was that some of our fourth and fifth graders moved to another school just before testing which affected our test scores negatively.

According to the higher powers of education at the state level, student enrollment and withdrawal from schools before the state test, was not an issue. It was explained to me that ALL students had the same opportunities to learn the skills required to take the state test. Where they went to school in the state, whether they moved from school to school, or that they moved to Johnson or out of Johnson before testing, was not a legitimate concern. So, our response to that was to plead our case to the parents by asking them not to move from Johnson School until after spring testing. When the new students enrolled in our school in the spring, before state testing, the teachers developed a plan of their own. They stayed after school, helped them with test taking strategies, and worked on getting their incomplete writing portfolios up to date and completed.

In the 1993-94 Johnson test years, the students showed improvement but didn't reach our state goal. Our test scores showed more improvement the next year and were closer to our goal. However, despite our efforts, the test scores continued to be the lowest in the county. The programs that we incorporated into the curriculum at the different grade levels impacted our test scores the following years, but it was a slow process to get our students where they needed to be on the state test.

Johnson School applied for, and received a Reading Recovery grant from the Fayette County Public Schools (FCPS) Equity Council, for non-reading first graders. Two teachers drove to Louisville, Kentucky, to be trained at the University Of Louisville since there was no Reading Recovery training available, locally. It was a very intense one on one reading program for our students. Every student who completed the program stayed on or above grade level in reading throughout their elementary years at Johnson.

One morning, one of the trained reading teachers brought a first grader up to the office. "Howie and I are going to visit my car for a few minutes. We'll be right back," she said. I looked out my office window and observed the teacher and student in the front seat of the teacher's parked car. Howie was turning the steering wheel left and right while jumping up and down in the driver's seat.

They returned to the office. The teacher exclaimed, "Howie's mother doesn't have a car, so when he gets to ride in a car, he's in the back seat. Howie learned what a steering wheel is and how it works. "Steering wheel" was a new word today in our lesson." Howie grinned big and shook his head in agreement.

Reading Recovery strategies, and the running record for evaluating students reading in the program, were taught to all the primary teachers. They used them in reading classes along with the Heath Whole Language approach. Thus, more students learned to read with comprehension. In my opinion, there needed to be a Reading Recovery teacher in every elementary school in the state. All children deserved to learn to read in the primary grades.

The Reading Recovery program was so important to Johnson School that it was featured in the Community Voice Newspaper. The well written article featured Johnson, Arlington, and Russell Schools each receiving seventy-five hundred dollars in donations on Unity Day from Baker Iron and Metal Company. A Reading Recovery lab was installed at Johnson for teacher training in Fayette County. The Community Voice was a local African American, free newspaper, which wrote about up and coming community events. Johnson School's events and activities were featured as well as those in other inner city schools.

Box It and Bag It Math was integrated into the primary curriculum.

It brought improved math scores. The <u>Opening Eyes with Math Program</u>, in collaboration with the computer lab teacher, special education resource classes, and all resource staff, improved the intermediate students' math scores. Teachers continued to be trained in ways to incorporate language arts into the math curriculum along with other necessary staff development.

In the intermediate grades, our goal was to move students from novice to apprentice, proficient, and on to distinguished. The language arts and reading teachers used the <u>Ginn of Canada </u>reading series, and novels from <u>BridgesI,</u> and <u>Bridges II.</u> The novels integrated reading with social studies. More students were reading the high interest books. Thematic Units were implemented in the reading and language arts program. Our science program was SCIS, (Science Curriculum of Integrated Systems) a "hands on" approach to teaching science. (Live organisms, crickets, frogs, and other living species on the food chain were observed, handled, and written about in every grade level).

All fourth and fifth graders wrote in journals daily. This helped the fourth graders with their writing portfolio pieces since they were used to writing everyday. To improve writing skills, a second computer was added to every classroom. This allowed students to write, and edit their work. The writing portfolio process was emphasized throughout the school year. Collaboration with the fourth and fifth grade teachers, and Title I teachers in reading, math, science, and social studies bolstered the academic progress of intermediate students.

Johnson School had an outstanding librarian who was knowledgeable in technology. Through her visionary talents, staff and students at all grade levels, had access to computerized information sources using the library media. When the computer lab was updated with new computers, the librarian installed the old ones in the library. This enabled students to have access to local public libraries to find books they needed for research. If the main library didn't have the book the student needed, other local libraries were searched.

The librarian ordered modems, CD roms, and various software packages for the students and staff to access a variety of national data bases. Some of these were electronic encyclopedias and other electronic information sources. The librarian received ongoing training in different software packages, then trained the staff and students.

Our students used computers everyday in their classrooms to do reading programs. They were in the computer lab twice weekly, in the library once weekly, and able to do research in the library during the morning before homeroom.

Several students were trained on the "Smart Board." This was an interactive computerized touch screen. Several students learned to do power point presentations on Smart Board for their classes. The librarian and the computer lab assistant worked together to provide innovative technology. Our staff and students really benefited from their expertise.

The computer lab assistant helped teachers keep records of their students' progress, and attendance with classroom computers, software, and laptop and notebook computers which could be used at home. Teachers continued technology training throughout the school year.

Johnson students became computer literate and were able to work independently on their classroom computers. This was important because most of our students didn't have a computer at home.

By purchasing Braille printers, optical character recognition devices, adaptive switches, interactive media, and laptop and notebook computers, we were able to enhance the learning skills of our special needs students. Special needs students who had laptops took them home and returned them to school the next day.

Our computer lab assistant started a fourth and fifth grade computer club. This club helped students learn how to clean a computer, install software, and put programs on the hard drive. They also learned how to troubleshoot simple problems that occurred on the computers in their classrooms.

The K.I.R.I.S. results showed our students were improving, but still not enough. In 1995-96 school year, we scored the lowest in the county on the KIRIS test, even though we showed improvement from the scores of the year before.

Additionally, the third grade test, C.T.B.S. (Comprehensive Test of Basic Skills), also was low, compared to other elementary schools. Two of the local newspaper staff wrote articles about Johnson School's low scores. They questioned my instructional leadership and rightly so. It looked like our third, fourth, and fifth grade students were "underachievers," compared to other county schools, and schools in the state. The staff and I were very frustrated. We felt that we were on the right track with our students' academic progress but knew we had to make it better. The question was how?

Two black community leaders in Lexington said that I needed more black teachers at Johnson who knew how to teach black students. What they didn't realize, and I didn't tell them, was that I already exceeded my quota of black teachers. There were five certified black teachers at Johnson School while there were other elementary schools which had one or none. All schools needed black teachers. I was grateful that we already had some of the best ones at Johnson.

Several of our classified employees were black and were effective role models for our students. Some of the black teachers called themselves African Americans. One teacher told me that she was not from Africa, she was from America, and wanted to be called black.

Some of the parents felt the same way. Eighty-seven year old Mrs. Price, our school neighbor, referred to her friends as colored. It depended on to whom you talked as to what word was used to describe the black race. Black parents enrolled their children and checked black on the enrollment form while others checked bi-racial. A few parents added African American before it was a choice on the enrollment form.

Johnson was fortunate to have many black and white student scholars who were school leaders. Students who had strong family support and were active in their churches, were especially strong role models. When our test scores the following year showed that Johnson School made its goal, one of the local black leaders called me to apologize for his negative remarks about my leadership. I accepted his apology because he truly cared about inner city black children. In my opinion, the problem was never about race, it was always about poverty.

Johnson students' academic success on the annual state test greatly improved by the next year. We felt the better scores were the result of the strategies of test taking throughout the school year in both the primary and intermediate grades. Weekly tests were given with weak areas being re-taught. Students' work, displayed in the halls, reflected academic increases in the areas of proficient and distinguished levels. Home visits were made the week before the state test. Our parents were reminded of the benefits of a good night's sleep and the importance of having the children eat breakfast at home or at school on testing days.

During the state test, the FRC provided snacks to the fourth and fifth graders during bathroom breaks. No talking was allowed but the snacks were greatly enjoyed!

During the 1996-97 school year, Johnson students' test scores improved by ten points, and we made our goal. We were so happy! The name of the state test called KIRIS was changed to C.A.T.S., or the Comprehensive Accountability Testing System.

Johnson students met their state goal on CATS, and in 1998-2000, we were in rewards! Our fourth and fifth grade students excelled on the state test.The third grade excelled on the CTBS (Comprehensive Test of Basic Skills). Our staff and families were very proud! Thanks to KERA, Johnson School students got a strong foundation in education from dedicated, well-trained teachers and staff.

* * *

The Southern Association of Colleges and Schools (SACS), sent a "School Renewal Team" to Johnson School every five years to make an on-site visit. All schools in Fayette County were visited by SACS. The site review team had three purposes:

- To confirm that the school was meeting the Southern Association Accreditation Standards
- To confirm that the school had an appropriate and ongoing School Improvement Plan, Consolidated Plan, Transformation Plan, or whatever the county called it for that year.
- To confirm that the School Improvement Plan had been effectively implemented.

The SACS committee wrote reports to the Accreditation Team in the following areas:

- Professional Development
- Planning and Budget
- Technology
- Site Based Decision Making Council (after KERA)
- Curriculum and Instruction
- School Climate and Social Committee
- Communication

The review team visited Johnson School, observed in classrooms, interviewed students and staff members, reviewed the school plan, and evaluated the school curriculum and the daily schedule. They wrote their commendations and recommendations which summarized their visit. It was a happy day when they informed the staff that we were in compliance with the Southern Association Standards. They were impressed with all the new programs and staff training. They spoke highly of the technology services in the computer lab and the library. All commented on the warmth and friendliness of the staff, students, and parents.

Mrs. Rebecca Wheat Hall Sutton

My mother was terminally ill during part of a school year. I made frequent trips to Charlotte, North Carolina to visit her at my oldest sister's home. (She was the care giver). My middle sister lived nearby in Concord, North Carolina which meant that all four of us could be together.

Mother's mind was sharp. We had many good talks. One time, my mother said, "I can't wait to see my mother and father, and your dad."

I replied, "Mother, please don't talk about the dead when you are here with me. You are still needed here."

Mother looked at me sternly and said, " If you think that, you're being selfish. I no longer have a purpose here on earth. You and your sisters have my good parts. It's time for me to go." I stood corrected and didn't say another word; I simply enjoyed what time we had left.

During an assembly at Johnson School one October, the school presented a box of letters from every student to me. These letters were addressed to my mother. I took them with me the following week-end while I visited her. I was overwhelmed and grateful for the wonderful letters. Mother and I read all of them. Some were religious, others were serious or funny. Several letters had drawings of flowers, houses, scenes, and stick people in them. They were signed with love from the students. There was one letter that mother held dear to her heart. It read, "Dear Betty, I heard you are dying and will go to heaven soon. When you get there, look up my grandmother, Sophie. She was my favorite grandmother when she was here on earth. I loved her very much and I know you will be good friends." Love, Monica. P.S. Your daughter is doing a good job as my principle."

During one visit, mother and I were talking about my new living room furniture. She asked, "Why are you buying furniture now?"

"Because my sons are grown and no longer living with me. Now I can buy nice things."

She replied, "You don't need more stuff. You can't take it with you. I've never seen a moving van behind a hearse!" She and I had a good laugh. She was full of life right up to the end. Once bedridden, she faded fast. I read her favorite passage, <u>Self Reliance</u>, by Ralph Waldo Emerson, before she lapsed into a coma and breathed her final breath. (Emerson was one of her favorite writers). When I lost my mother, I lost my childhood. She was the only one who loved me unconditionally. I think of her often.

Rebecca Wheat Hall Sutton

Magnet School/Community School

During the KERA years (1991-2001), Johnson School incorporated several innovative programs for the students and staff which helped support academic improvement on the state test.

During the 1990's, redistricting was a hot topic for many parents in our school district. New subdivisions were being built on the south side of town which created overcrowding in several of the south end schools. The inner city schools, on the other hand, had low enrollments, and plenty of space for south end students, if needed.

By the 1990's the magnet school concept had evolved into a few schools such as The School for the Creative and Performing Arts (SCAPA), and Maxwell Elementary Spanish Immersion Program. However, certain requirements for admission included auditions for SCAPA which were part of the enrollment and admission process. Magnet schools were allowed to have choices on curriculum and who would attend.

Johnson Elementary staff was told by the District, to write a program to become a magnet school. There was discussion about Johnson being a technology magnet school. When we sent a proposal to central office, the magnet committee felt our proposal was too basic to attract elementary students from the overcrowded south end.

As discussion continued about Johnson becoming a magnet school with our Site Based Decision Making Council and staff, I became worried that becoming a magnet would change everything we had worked so hard to achieve.

First, no program which could be incorporated into the existing academic school environment, improved as it was, would bring middle/upper middle class students to the inner city. Middle and upper middle class families bought houses in the south end to have their children go to school there, not to have their children bused to inner city elementary schools.

In Johnson P.T.A. meetings, the parents discussed becoming a magnet school or continuing to be a community school. The parents voted to remain the way we were. The Site Based Council discussed the magnet school proposal and voted unanimously for Johnson to remain a community school.

Next, nearly four hundred parents and community members signed a petition asking the Fayette County Board of Education to allow Johnson School to remain a neighborhood school. Several parents and I went to the board meeting with the petition in hand. A few parents took the podium and spoke. The Board voted to leave Johnson as a community school!

There was a very successful magnet middle school near Johnson on Fourth Street. It was called Lexington Traditional Magnet Middle School. Students had to be on or above grade level to enroll there. Most of the students who attended LTMS were bussed from south end schools. Conversely, the majority of inner city students didn't meet the criteria. They were bused out of the inner city instead of being able to walk to their local middle school.

Healthy Kids Clinic

An energetic, innovative pediatrician, Dr. Thomas Young, (real name), was in a meeting that I attended in 1995. I was lamenting my concerns about health problems that my students faced. I shared that Johnson School badly needed a full time nurse.

Dr. Young said, "It sounds like you need a health clinic in your school."

Then, he made it happen!

The school applied for a collaborative grant which became a reality in 1996.The Johnson Healthy Kids Clinic received funding from the University of Kentucky Childrens' Hospital, and Central Baptist Hospital, in collaboration with the Lexington-Fayette County Health Department, and Fayette County School system. Our clinic opened in January1996. It housed a doctor, a nurse, and a family mental health therapist. Partitions separated spaces for a small examining room, therapy room, and areas for receptionist and patients.

The goals of the Healthy Kids Clinic were to improve educational outcomes by promoting healthy behaviors. This meant improving the physical, mental, and dental health of our students.

The clinic provided exams, immunizations, sick and injury care, health education to students and parents, mental health counseling, and dental screening for the students. Positive changes in our school were increased school attendance and healthy students in the classroom. Our clinic was one of three nationally recognized as a school clinic model.

Once the clinic was in place at Johnson, we could enroll a student, update needed immunizations, and send the student to class. In the past, the parents had to take the child to the health department to get necessary immunizations during which the child was counted absent from school.

Thanks to the Healthy Kids Clinic, parents became more health conscious about their children. Serious health problems were diagnosed earlier and treated. Head lice was under control and was no longer an attendance issue as it had been in previous years.

Johnson students went to the Dental Clinic, at the University of Kentucky, every Friday. Different students went every week except for a few who had severe dental issues. Over one hundred students were seen at the Dental Clinic on a regular basis throughout the school year. Tooth cavities were prevalent among the students who were four to eleven years of age. Some of their mothers and fathers had few or no teeth.

A very important component of the Healthy Kids Clinic was counseling. This was especially helpful to mothers who were victims of domestic violence. Several parents met weekly in a support group. The counseling and support groups greatly benefited both mothers and children.

If a student needed testing for Attention Deficit Disorder, he could be tested in the clinic by a doctor with parent permission. If the student needed medication, the doctor prescribed it. However, most often, alternatives to medication were discussed and implemented.

One day a third grader, Raymond, was sent to the office for going to the bathroom every fifteen minutes. The teacher thought he might be playing in the bathroom instead of using the facility.

" Raymond, are you using the bathroom or are you playing in there?" I asked.

He replied, " I have to pee all the time, Miss Show. I can't help it."

I said, "Raymond, if you are going to the bathroom that much, you need to see the doctor in the clinic."

Usually if I said that to a student, he'd protest, and want to return to class.

Raymond said, "O.K." and walked with me to the clinic.

I told the doctor about Raymond's frequent bathroom trips. He was tested and diagnosed with diabetes. His parents were contacted by way of an immediate home visit and Raymond was admitted to the hospital. Thank goodness the clinic was in the school!

A very valuable team at Johnson was the S.A.T. (Student Assistance Team). Any concern a teacher or parent had over a student's behavior, academics, health issues, or family life was sent to the SAT. A meeting was then scheduled. The people who were present at all the meetings were the principal, the guidance counselor, the teacher, the parent, a doctor, and a nurse. The teacher expressed problems occurring in class, the parent spoke about home issues, I discussed misbehavior if the student was sent to the office, and the counselor talked about any counseling concerns. The energy in the room was powerful!

The doctor listened and gave input from his medical background. He gave advice that we as educators didn't think about. In one meeting, the parent told about her son's misbehavior at home. That same behavior had been observed by staff at school. After listening to all of us express our views about the student, the doctor said, "You all have talked about the symptoms of depression. I need to see the student after this meeting." We were dumbfounded. He was absolutely right. We were not able to see the "big picture" with the student at all.

The doctor gave the student a medical evaluation while the mother was present in the clinic. He was very depressed. The mother, father, and child had weekly therapy sessions. Improvement was seen both at home and at school. After weeks of therapy, the student's grades improved. The sessions brought the family much closer. They were able to talk openly with each other.

Some of the abused mothers found positive solutions through therapy and their children seemed happier at school. Support groups for women were formed in the FRC.

Being able to meet childrens' health needs at school was one of the greatest gifts we gave the students at Johnson. Our families became more health conscious about nutrition and exercise and our attendance improved.

The parents appreciated the clinic because they didn't have to walk a mile to the health department or take their child to the hospital emergency room during the school day.

The "Health Fair" at Johnson School began out of the need to educate parents and the community on how to be healthy. Different organizations had booths for nutrition, health issues like diabetes, blood pressure checks, and other health problems. Healthy snacks were provided while young and old dance groups performed. It was well attended on a Saturday and became an annual event.

As principal of Johnson School, I was proud of our students' academic achievements and all of the programs that we put in place for them and their families. However, I was most proud of fighting for and receiving a Healthy Kids Clinic.

Thank you, Dr. Thomas Young, for making it happen!

Community School That Never Closes

Margaret Meade once said, "Never doubt that a small group of thoughtful committed citizens can change the world. Indeed it's the only thing that ever has."

The Community School That Never Closes (CSNC), was established in November of 1996 in response to inner city residents' pleas for help to drastically change life in their community.

A group of residents, and their leader, Susan North (MSW), with my assistance from Johnson School, started the movement. CSNC was housed in a portable building on our school property, beside the school.

CSNC formed partnerships in the private and public sector to provide services for inner city residents. The goal was to start new programs where needed and bring existing programs into the inner city community.

The residents who served on the advisory committee identified the following needs:

- Improved access to more educational opportunities for children and adults
- Access to free health services and medication for the uninsured
- Access to computer training and computers for the students' homes
- Child care services available twenty-four hours a day, seven days a week
- Job training leading to job placement and higher paying jobs
- Basic needs including help with rent, utilities, clothing, food, and housing
- Support services to help women transition off of welfare

- Day, evening, and week-end programs to keep children off the streets and out of trouble

CSNC was an education, human services and economic development organization. The mission was community revitalization through education, workforce development, and the promotion of new businesses in the inner city.

The business was changing people's lives by training them to be productive members of the workforce and larger society, and by providing them with opportunities to excel.

CSNC was open six days per week for twelve months, annually.

An ongoing problem for Johnson parents without health insurance was lack of access to medical services. Parents were glad that their children could go to the school health clinic but wanted something similar for themselves. Untreated health issues were major hurdles to be overcome in order for the uninsured to live productive lives.

CSNC solved this problem through a collaborative partnership with St. Joseph Hospital. The hospital had purchased a brand new bus which was adapted to become a mobile medical clinic. Community residents seeking health services waited each Monday afternoon in the CSNC office. The mobile clinic arrived at 4:00p.m. and stayed until the last patient was seen around 9:00p.m.

A newsletter from St. Joseph Hospital stated, "In accordance with the Christian mission of Saint Joseph Hospital, and in an effort to improve access to healthcare in a positive, dignified, clinical atmosphere, Saint Joseph will operate a state of the art mobile clinic. The clinic will be in a 40 ft., self-contained RV which will travel to community sites. Population sites were identified for residents who were underserved for health care and human services."

The first sites were:
- Johnson Elementary School
- Saint Peter Claver Parrish and surrounding community
- Gainesway Plaza/ Centre Parkway and surrounding community
- The migrant worker in Cardinal Valley area.
- Trinity Baptist Church and surrounding community

The mobile medical service was directed by a physician from St. Joseph Hospital and was staffed by a family nurse practitioner, a registered nurse practitioner, a social worker, and volunteers. In addition, physicians on staff at St. Joseph Hospital volunteered their services. Emphasis for the mobile clinic was on developing linkages with community resources, including Baby Health Services Inc., the health department, Comprehensive Care, the Cabinet for Health Services, and area churches and neighborhood associations."

One time, a homeless man arrived at the Johnson site complaining of a severe pain in his side. The doctor diagnosed him with acute appendicitis. He needed emergency surgery and was operated on that evening at St. Joseph Hospital.

Many Johnson families and community people used the Johnson site on Monday evenings; more people were seen at our site than all of the other four sites put together!

Thank you, St. Joseph Hospital.

* * *

Through an agreement with Transylvania University, twenty-five intermediate students in third, fourth, and fifth grades attended Johnson, every Saturday from 9:00 a.m.-12:00 noon. Breakfast snacks were served and cultural enrichment activities were taught by ten university students. Johnson students learned about different world cultures while global games and activities were played in the gymnasium. Crafts were taught and students took their finished work home. A trip to the Transylvania University campus was a highlight for the students.

One Saturday morning, a university student came into my office and said, "I came here to give back to you and Johnson students. You and the teachers at Johnson helped me get to college. Now it's my turn to help you."

I choked back the tears and hugged Craig, a former Johnson student, who was now a Transylvania student volunteering in Saturday School. Throughout the morning activities,I observed our students hanging around Craig as he taught them. It brought back memories of when Craig was a student here; how excited he was when the University of Kentucky athletes visited his class several years ago.

Later in the school year, Georgetown University volunteered some of their students to teach during Saturday School. Johnson children benefited from the interaction with both universities all year long.

* * *

G.E.D. (General Education Diploma) classes were taught to adults on Saturday from 9:00 a.m.-12:00 noon. Several adults and students, who dropped out of school at sixteen years of age, came every Saturday for class and finished the program.

"Operation Read" was available on Saturday mornings for any adult who wanted to learn how to read. A trained specialist taught the class. All of the programs were free to both adults and students.

* * *

Another opportunity provided by CSNC was bi-weekly computer classes for adults. After sixteen hours of instruction, donated computers were installed in the residents' homes.

* * *

The "Welfare to Work" training classes had a 100% success rate in moving women from welfare to corporate America. Bank One, in Lexington, sponsored the six month training course for women who were parents at Johnson School. The class met weekly from 4:00-7:00 p.m. in the school library. The women were taught by a bank official. They learned how to become a bank teller and had the opportunity to advance to higher positions in the bank. When they increased their skills and knowledge of banking and passed the final examination, they were honored in a special ceremony which was held in the school gymnasium. A five-day wardrobe was donated to each of the graduates in order to provide them with a professional look for their first week on the job. Thank you, Bank One.

* * *

CSNC, in partnership with the Department for Community Based Services, provided a public assistance worker on-site who served forty families each year. A child protective services worker was located in the same building. The CPS worker provided prevention and intervention services. The workers were also available in the summer months when school was not in session.

CSNC, with the YMCA, opened a child day care across the street from Johnson School. It was called Jane's Place. Donated funds to support it were given in honor of a community person's deceased wife. The day care was needed by mothers who were employed or seeking employment in the community.

The Renaissance Program was an after school educational opportunity for interested Johnson students which was funded by the CSNC. Sixty participants attended classes for two hours, after every regular school day. Its program started after school dismissed. Parts of the curriculum included French, accelerated math, literacy, and chorus. These classes were taught by professionals in each field. After a year in the program, positive improvements in reading and math levels of our students were realized.

Inner city residents and Johnson parents decided that CSNC needed a bigger facility to house all of its programs and activities. Two architects, Ron Witte and John Dehart, met with school and community folks to learn what was needed in the community center.

They designed a unique building to house all of the programs and activities that the citizens wanted.

Community School that Never Closes impacted our community families by providing many needed services. Thank you, Susan North.

Bank boosts women's careers

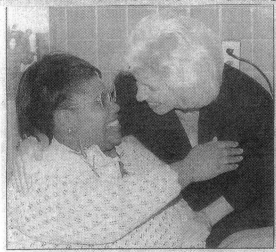

Program coordinator Susan North, right, congratulated Stephanie Drake, who is off welfare and working at a Bank One branch.

Mayor Pam Miller said the program allows people to change the way they live.

Primary Pilot Program

In the primary grades, there were effective reading programs for kindergarten through third grade students. The emphasis was on reading and reading components, for two and one- half hours each day. This was beneficial to the students. With twenty-four students in each class, the teachers were concerned that they were not able to spend time with those who needed extra assistance.

Primary students needed to read fluently by the third grade or risk being poor readers throughout elementary school. There were three other inner city schools with the same concern. All four shared many of the same students over the years. Despite the fact that some students moved often, within a school year, many students still lived in various low income areas, downtown.

A possible solution to the need for additional time that teachers could spend teaching primary students to read, was to lower the ratio of teachers to students to 15:1, rather than 24:1. Parents were encouraged to keep their students at Johnson even if they moved. The District provided a bus to pick up out of district children and bring them to Johnson, each day.

In March 1998, a Pilot Proposal titled: Increasing Student Achievement Via Primary Staffing and Reduced Mobility was created. In the proposal, a staffing committee recommended to the superintendent that primary classes be reduced to a staffing ratio of 15:1 without any teacher assistants, except for kindergarten, where assistants were required by law.

All four inner city schools discussed the pilot program with their SBDM Councils and staff.

An addition to pilot program was The Mobility Project. The project goal was to increase student achievement by keeping students in the same school for six years. A bus provided transportation for students who moved out-of-area.

The proposal stated that all four schools would work collaboratively with their Family Resource Centers to prepare and distribute educational materials to parents which explained the benefits of their children staying in one school all year. School staff would attempt to counsel parents as they enrolled their children, and, before exiting the school, if they moved. The document also insured that District staff and school staff would work with school transportation to ensure continuity of attendance to the same school all year long.

In the fall of 1998-99 school year, the Primary Pilot Program began. The staff and students enjoyed the small class size. The local paper wrote about the Primary Pilot Program and interviewed some of our students.

One student said, "My teacher talks to me all day long and I get all my work done."

Another student remarked, "I have my own space and more space in class than I ever had. We're like a family."

The primary second and third grade teachers felt that they were more effective with smaller class.. A few of them missed their assistants but liked the program overall.

Improved results in the students' reading scores, at the end of the year, showed the pilot program was a success.

Year Around Calendar

In 1999, Johnson School became a <u>Year Around Calendar School.</u> The new school calendar featured four quarters. Each quarter lasted nine weeks with 2, two-week breaks. The new calendar featured six weeks of summer vacation. Our new school year began two weeks before most of the other elementary schools. Arlington Elementary School had adopted the new calendar the year before. Mary Todd Elementary School started the same year as Johnson.

Every nine weeks there was a scheduled break in the calendar. The first week of break was for summer school which was for at risk students. Everyone was on break the second week.

The Johnson Site Based Council voted for the <u>Year Around Calendar</u> because they felt the summer vacation was too long for our students to be out of school. They also believed that the students forgot what they had learned the previous year. This meant that a lot of time had to be spent during the new school year on review and re-teaching information that should have been retained.

After one year of being on the alternate calendar, the students progressed academically and retained most of what was taught the previous year. Teachers were able to start the new curriculum earlier because the students were more prepared to learn new material. The <u>Year Around Calendar</u> was a success at Johnson Elementary School.

Governor Patton Visits Johnson School

Kentucky Governor Paul Patton and Lieutenant Governor Steve Henry visited Johnson School in May 1999.This was the first year we were in rewards on the CATS Test. Early in the morning, before they arrived, state security men did a check of the classrooms and hallways in the building.

"Who are those men?" one student asked.

"Those are security men who protect the governor and lieutenant governor at all times. They have to check to make sure everything is safe before the governor comes into the school building," I replied.

"We can keep him safe," another student said.

"I know you can but these men are paid to do the job," I said.

Governor Patton was supposed to do a quick walk through, give a short speech, and leave. Many parents, staff, and guests were in the library when he arrived. Student greeters welcomed him and Lt. Governor Henry, and escorted them into the library. A student presented a Johnson tee shirt to the governor, who made a short speech, and walked down the hall to the classrooms.

While visiting the computer lab, Governor Patton was impressed with the students working on the computers. One student even took his hand to show him a writing program.

When the governor walked down the hall, I noticed two fifth grade boys walking on each side of him. One of the boys whispered, "We are protecting him."

Governor Patton was escorted downstairs as lunch was being served. When he saw the menu, he decided to have lunch with the students. Our cafeteria workers knew the governor would be visiting. They had prepared meal hoping that he'd stay for lunch.

The menu was fried chicken, green beans, cooked cabbage and carrots, mashed potatoes and gravy, hot rolls, and Derby Pie. The pie was made especially for him.

The governor and his staff, as well as parents and guests, all ate lunch together with the fourth and fifth graders. Afterwards, pictures were taken of everyone with Governor Patton, including the cafeteria workers. Several boys told the governor that they wanted to be security people when they grew up. He told them they could be governor, too!

Governor Paul Patton and Johnson Students in the Cafeteria in 1999

International Welcoming School Award and National Title I Parent Involvement Award

In 1995, Johnson Elementary School was awarded the <u>Welcoming School</u> Award by the Partnership of Kentucky Schools.

To receive the award, a school had to be committed to involving parents, families, and the community at large in its efforts to reach higher learning standards for students. This involvement required participation, support, and a visitor friendly climate with everyone in and around the school.

In 1999, Johnson School was awarded the state <u>Invitational Education Award.</u> During the 2000-01 school year, Johnson School was awarded the <u>International Inviting School Award.</u>

Invitational Education (Purkey and Novak, 1988,1996) is a "Five-P" approach to school improvement:

1. <u>People</u>-How do we see ourselves and our students relating to each other to improve the quality of life for the people in the school; how do we nurture caring relationships to improve human potential?

2. <u>Places</u>-How do we examine our school facility and grounds and find ways to enhance the total physical environment of the school; is this a place where people want to be and learn?

3. <u>Policies</u>- in reviewing our policies, can we identify rules and regulations that may not be inviting and make them more encouraging and evolving; showing the spirit of the school to be more inviting?

4. <u>Programs</u>-in planning or revising our programs, we can find

ways to create more meaningful connections with our students, the curriculum, and the world around us, while continuing to have high expectations for our students to be successful.

5. Processes-How we go about the processes we employ to transform our school need to be inviting. How we go about creating a more exciting, satisfying, and enriching school becomes as important as defining the inviting school we want to become.

Once we received the "1999 Inviting School Award," we applied for the" International Inviting School Award " in 2000-01. Johnson School submitted a picture notebook addressing all five areas above. We showed the committee, through pictures and words, how much we had improved. It was a winner!

Johnson was honored to receive the award. The staff worked hard, every year, to make the school an inviting place for students, parents, visitors, and guests, while maintaining a high academic atmosphere for the students. A huge white wall- to- wall banner was installed in the front foyer that read, "Striving For Excellence In an Atmosphere of learning and love". Anyone who entered the school building saw the sign and felt welcome.

* * *

That same year, 2000-2001, Johnson School received the National Title I Award for Parent Involvement. This was an award given on the federal level. Anytime a parent entered the school for an event, a conference, to volunteer, or to visit, they signed in the office or Family Resource Center. Signing in on every visit was a successful way of measuring parent involvement in multiple areas.

Retirement

June 1, 2001, I retired from the Fayette County School System after 35 years in education. I enjoyed my years first, as a physical education teacher, and later as principal of Johnson Elementary.

I loved going to work everyday. It was that simple! I had a passion about improving all children's education. I believed that I could make a difference in the lives of the students.

It is my hope that this memoir will show administrators and teachers, who work in the inner city schools, throughout in the United States, that all things are possible when people work together for the good of children.

Most of all, I hope this memoir demonstrates the tireless dedication and determination that educators devote to helping students reach their fullest academic potential.